A wonderful poem for my
wonderful nephew, Adam.
Maybe Ethan will like it
someday too.

Love,
Louise

The Song of Hiawatha

A. Willmore Sc.

The Song of Hiawatha
by Henry Wadsworth Longfellow
with illustrations from designs by
Frederic Remington

Bounty Books

New York

Copyright © 1982 by Crown Publishers, Inc.
All rights reserved.

This edition published by Bounty Books,
distributed by Crown Publishers, Inc.

Manufactured in the United States of America

Library of Congress Cataloging in Publication Data

Longfellow, Henry Wadsworth, 1807–1882.
The song of Hiawatha.

Originally published, 1968.
1. Indians of North America—Poetry.
I. Remington, Frederic, 1861–1909.   II. Title.
PS2267.A1   1982   811′.3   82-1159
                                       AACR2

ISBN: 0-517-001977

n m l k j i h

The Song of Hiawatha

FOREWORD

More than 125 years ago—before the Civil War—Henry Wadsworth Longfellow brought to the attention of the world some of the beautiful stories and legends of Native Americans in his epic poem *The Song of Hiawatha*. Despite the poem's immense popularity and the widespread controversy it created, the culture and legends of these people have not received the attention and study they deserve. And it is still possible to find Native Americans portrayed as villainous, blood-thirsty savages in popular entertainments.

Much has been done, however, to change this image and to correct this lack of knowledge. Long-fellow was certainly a major force in educating people about the native inhabitants of this country. He wrote many works about them throughout his entire life, ever mindful of what they had suffered from the white man. *The Courtship of Miles Standish,* "Eliot's Oak," and "The Revenge of Rain-in-the-Face" are but a few examples.

When *The Song of Hiawatha* was published in 1855, it received much praise and much criticism. One critic from the *Boston Traveller* chose to display his ignorance and lack of intelligence:

> We cannot but express our regret that our own pet national poet should not have selected as the theme of his muse something higher and better than the silly legends of the savage aborigines. His poem does not awaken one sympathetic throb; it does not touch a single truth; and rendered into prose, *Hiawatha* would be a mess of the most childish nonsense that ever dropped from human pen.

Even the admiring critic Nathan Haskell Dole, in his introduction to an 1898 edition of the poem, betrayed a condescending attitude to the original material when he says that Longfellow was successful at "[transmuting] the crude material of Indian folktale into the finished, graceful poem that appeals to the heart of the most cultivated, and yet has the fragrance of the primitive woods."

One early pioneer who *did* believe in the importance of Indian culture was Henry Rowe Schoolcraft, an American ethnologist who first visited Sault Ste. Marie, a frontier settlement in northern

Michigan, in 1820. He lived there among the Ojibways for thirty years studying their culture and way of life. His published works were Longfellow's source for most of the legends in *Hiawatha*.

This reprint of the poem, with the Introductory Note and the Frederic Remington illustrations, was originally published in 1891. Since that time much new light has been shed on Native American legends and culture. The Introductory Note tells of Longfellow using "Manabozho's other...name," Hiawatha. These, however, were two different people: Manabozho was a trickster in the legends of the Ojibway tribe; Hiawatha was a real person, an Onondaga chief, whose deeds became legendary. A wise leader, he is believed to have been instrumental in forming a powerful organization of tribes called the Five Nations. Adventures of these and other figures are attributed to Hiawatha in Longfellow's poem, but the poet was not attempting to relate the authentic tales with strict attention to accuracy. He took several legends and wove them into a beautiful tapestry: the life and adventures of a composite character named Hiawatha.

The poem is a marvelous panorama of adventure and drama, humor and tragedy. Hiawatha grows up under the wise tutelage of his grandmother, Nokomis, daughter of the Moon. There are tales of Hiawatha's victories over his foes—even his own father, the West-Wind. There are "how

and why" legends such as how maize was dis-
covered and how the woodpecker got his red top.
Stories of Hiawatha killing monstrous beasts re-
mind us of European myths of heroic knights
slaying hideous dragons. A haunting tale of ghosts
from the land of the dead sends shivers through us.

As the epic approaches its end, Hiawatha's
world retreats into shadows and darkness. His
friends Kwasind and Chibiabos are killed. A great
famine takes his wife, Minnehaha. The white man
arrives. Though Hiawatha welcomes his arrival,
he knows it marks the beginning of the end. The
wise warrior must travel westward and die in his
own world, on his own terms.

Throughout the whole, there is Longfellow's
poetic touch, his skilled craftsmanship, his love of
nature and mankind, and his love for the culture of
the people native to this country. His epic poem
fires our imagination and reveals magical myths
and legends that awake in us a spirit that we share
with peoples from all over the world—a spirit that
we have shared since the beginning of time.

DOUGLAS DESHIELD

The Song of Hiawatha

INTRODUCTORY NOTE

Evangeline, published in 1847, was followed by *The Golden Legend* in 1851, and that by *Hiawatha* in 1855. The general purpose to make use of Indian material appears to have been in the poet's mind for some time, but the conception as finally wrought was formed in the summer of 1854. He writes in his diary under date of June 22, " I have at length hit upon a plan for a poem on the American Indians, which seems to me the right one and the only. It is to weave together their beautiful traditions into a whole. I have hit upon a measure, too, which I think the

right and only one for such a theme." A few
days before, he had been reading with great
delight the Finnish epic *Kalevala*, and this
poem suggested the measure and may well
have reminded him also of the Indian legends,
which have that likeness to the Finnish that
springs from a common intellectual stage of
development and a general community of habits and occupation.

An interest in the Indians had long been
felt by Mr. Longfellow, and in his early plans
for prose sketches tales about the Indians had
a place. He had seen a few of the straggling
remainder of the Algonquins in Maine, and
had read Heckewelder while in college; he
had witnessed the spectacle of Black Hawk
and his Sioux on Boston Common; and a few
years before he had made the acquaintance of
the fine-tempered Kah-ge-ga-gah'bowh, the
Ojibway chief, and had entertained him at
his house, trusting not unlikely that he might
derive from the Indian helpful suggestion.

No sooner had his floating ideas of a work
taken shape than he was eager to put his plans
into execution. "I could not help this evening," he wrote June 25, "making a beginning
of *Manabozho*, or whatever the poem is to be

called. His adventures will form the theme,
at all events;" and the next day; "look over
Schoolcraft's great book on the Indians; three
huge quartos, ill-digested, and without any
index. Write a few lines of the poem." His
authority for the legends and the material
generally of his poem was in the main Schoolcraft's work, with probably the same author's
more literary composition, *Algic Researches*,
and Heckewelder's narrative. He soon took
Manabozho's other and more euphonic name,
Hiawatha, into his service, and gave himself
up to a thorough enjoyment of the task.
"Worked at *Hiawatha*," he wrote on the
31st of the month, "as I do more or less every
day. It is purely in the realm of fancy.
After tea, read to the boys the Indian story
of *The Red Swan*." "*Hiawatha*," he wrote
again in October, "occupies and delights me.
Have I no misgivings about it? Yes, sometimes. Then the theme seizes me and hurries
me away, and they vanish." His misgivings
took a concrete shape a few days later, when
he read aloud to a friend some pages of his
work. "He fears the poem will want human
interest. So does F. So does the author. I
must put a live, beating heart into it."

Mr. Longfellow began writing *Hiawatha*, as we have seen, June 25, 1854. It was finished March 29, 1855, and published November 10. It is doubtful if the poet wrote any of his longer works with more abandonment, with more thorough enjoyment of his task, with a keener sense of the originality of his venture, and by consequence, with more perplexity when he thought of his readers. He tried the poem on his friends more freely than had been customary with him, and with varied results. His own mind, as he neared the test of publication, wavered a little in its moods. " Proof sheets of *Hiawatha*," he wrote in June, 1855. " I am growing idiotic about this song, and no longer know whether it is good or bad ; " and later still : " In great doubt about a canto of *Hiawatha*, — whether to retain or suppress it. It is odd how confused one's mind becomes about such matters from long looking at the same subject."

No sooner was the poem published than its popularity was assured, and it was subjected to the most searching tests. It was read by public readers to large audiences, and a few years later was set to music by Stoepel and given at the Boston Theatre with explanatory

readings by Matilda Heron. It was paro-
died, — one of the surest signs of popularity,
and it lived its parodies down, a surer sign still
of intrinsic uncopyableness. It was criticised
with heated words, and made the occasion for
controversy. The elemental nature of the
poetry led to vehement charges of plagiarism,
and altogether the poet found himself in the
midst of a violent war of words which recalled
his experience with *Hyperion*. He felt keenly
the unreasonableness of the attack upon his
honesty in the charge that he had borrowed
metre and incidents both from the *Kalevala*.
He made no secret of the suggestion of the
metre, — he had used an acknowledged form,
which was not exclusively Finnish; and as for
the legends, he openly confessed his indebted-
ness to Schoolcraft in the notes to the poem.
Referring to an article in a Washington paper,
embodying these charges, he wrote to Mr.
Sumner, December 3, 1855 : —

This is truly one of the greatest literary outrages I
ever heard of. But I think it is done mainly to show
the learning of the writer. . . . He will stand finally in
the position of a man who makes public assertions which
he cannot substantiate. You see what the charge of im-
itation amounts to, by the extracts given. As to my
having " taken many of the most striking incidents of

the Finnish Epic and transferred them to the American Indians " — it is absurd.   I can give chapter and verse for these legends.   Their chief value is that they *are* Indian legends.   I know the *Kalevala* very well ; and that some of its legends *resemble* the Indian stories preserved by Schoolcraft is very true.   But the idea of making me responsible for that is too ludicrous.

Freiligrath wrote to him with reference to a discussion going on in the London *Athenæum* over the metre : " The very moment I looked into the book I exclaimed, —

Launawatar, Frau die alte,

and was laughing with you again over the pages of the *Finnische Runen*, as thirteen years ago on the Rhine. The characteristic feature, which shows that you have fetched the metre from the Finns, is the *parallelism* adopted so skilfully and so gracefully in *Hia-watha*." In a note in his diary upon this letter, Mr. Longfellow added : " He does not seem to be aware that the parallelism, or repetition, is as much the characteristic of Indian as of Finnish song."

Freiligrath translated *Hiawatha*, as he had other of Mr. Longfellow's poems, and in acknowledging the receipt of the translation, the poet wrote, January 29, 1857 : —

It is admirable, this translation of yours, as I knew it would be from the samples sent before. A thousand and a thousand thanks for it, and may Cotta pay you, as the broker paid Guzman de Alfarache, in money *sahumada, y lavada con agua de ángeles.* A passage was changed in the proofs which I sent to Bogue [the English publisher], and which he promised to hand to you. It is in the description of the sturgeon. This was changed to —

> As above him Hiawatha
> In his birch canoe came sailing,
> With his fishing line of cedar, —

because the sturgeon, I found, was never guilty of the crime of frightening or eating his fellow fishes. . . . What you say, in the preface, of the close of the poem is very true. The contact of Saga and History is too sudden. But how could I remedy it unless I made the poem very much longer? I felt the clash and concussion, but could not prevent nor escape it.

Meanwhile the book had an unexampled sale, and the letters which the poet received from Emerson, Hawthorne, Parsons, Taylor, and others showed the judgment passed upon his work by those whose poetic perception was not blunted by habits of professional criticism nor taken captive by mere novelty. Several years after, a translation into Latin of a portion of the poem was made for use as a school-book, by Professor Francis W. Newman. Mr. Samuel Longfellow in his Life of

the poet relates the following anecdote, illus-
trative of the popularity of the poem : —

A lady relates that, passing one day a jeweller's win-
dow in New York, her attention was arrested by hearing
from a crowd gathered before it a voice in unmistaka-
ble brogue, saying, "Shure, and that's for Hiawatha."
The speaker was a ragged Irish laborer, unshaven and
unshorn. She looked, and saw a silver boat with the
figure of an Indian standing in the prow. "That must
be," continued the speaker, "for a prisintation to the
poet Longfellow ; thim two lines cut on the side of the
boat is from his poethry." "That is fame," said the
friend to whom she told the story.

A word with regard to the illustrations.
The full-page photogravures are designed by
Mr. Remington to serve directly as accom-
paniments to the poem, and he has followed
the poet in using a certain freedom of treatment. For as Mr. Longfellow was more careful of the Indian type than exact in a con-
sistent portraiture of one personage, and used
his imagination to emphasize the central
truths of his poetic interpretation of Indian
life, rather than sought to follow scrupulously
the lines of the archæologist, so the artist,
reading the poem, has made a series of
pictures which have a basis of reality from
his long and close study of the Indian in

many situations, but sometimes are fanciful
in their treatment. Mr. Longfellow made
Indian pictures in verse and Mr. Remington
has made Indian pictures in design, studying
to make them correspond in spirit with the
poet's conception, but not attempting to
square the poet's description with the actual
realities of Indian life as he knows it by
observation.

The pen-and-ink drawings which decorate
the margin of the text are, on the other hand,
faithful representations of a large number of
actual objects, in use among Indian tribes, or
associated with their life. Most of these objects are mentioned in the poem, but many
are not, for the artist was desirous of making
this collection of drawings a museum of Indian curiosities, and in pursuit of his object
he has drawn both from his own large accu-
mulation of material obtained in observations
made during frequent intercourse with Indian tribes, and from a diligent study of objects as stored in museums or pictured by
trustworthy artists. A few of the objects
which accompany the Notes are later in date
than the time of the poem, and show the
presence of the white man. The artist, in a

word, has studied to depict actual objects,
indifferent to the possible criticism that in so
doing he has departed from a strict regard
to the time of the poem.   His larger purpose
has been to make these pen-and-ink sketches
a storehouse of information regarding Indian
life in its varied details.

Contents

Contents and List of Illustrations

[Photogravures executed by A. W. Elson & Co., Boston]

Introduction

The Song of Hiawatha

INTRODUCTION

SHOULD you ask me, whence these stories?
Whence these legends and traditions,
With the odors of the forest,
With the dew and damp of meadows,
With the curling smoke of wigwams,
With the rushing of great rivers,
With their frequent repetitions,
And their wild reverberations,
As of thunder in the mountains?
   I should answer, I should tell you,
" From the forests and the prairies,
From the great lakes of the Northland,
From the land of the Ojibways,

From the land of the Dacotahs,
From the mountains, moors, and fen-lands
Where the heron, the Shuh-shuh-gah,
Feeds among the reeds and rushes.
I repeat them as I heard them
From the lips of Nawadaha,
The musician, the sweet singer."

    Should you ask where Nawadaha
Found these songs so wild and wayward,
Found these legends and traditions,
I should answer, I should tell you,
" In the bird's-nests of the forest,
In the lodges of the beaver,
In the hoof-prints of the bison,
In the eyry of the eagle !

    " All the wild-fowl sang them to him,
In the moorlands and the fen-lands,
In the melancholy marshes ;
Chetowaik, the plover, sang them,
Mahng, the loon, the wild-goose, Wawa,
The blue heron, the Shuh-shuh-gah,
And the grouse, the Mushkodasa ! "

    If still further you should ask me,
Saying, " Who was Nawadaha ?
Tell us of this Nawadaha,"
I should answer your inquiries
Straightway in such words as follow.

"In the Vale of Tawasentha,
In the green and silent valley,
By the pleasant water-courses,
Dwelt the singer Nawadaha.
Round about the Indian village
Spread the meadows and the corn-fields,
And beyond them stood the forest,
Stood the groves of singing pine-trees,
Green in Summer, white in Winter,
Ever sighing, ever singing.

"And the pleasant water-courses,
You could trace them through the valley,
By the rushing in the Spring-time,
By the alders in the Summer,
By the white fog in the Autumn,
By the black line in the Winter;
And beside them dwelt the singer,
In the Vale of Tawasentha,
In the green and silent valley.

"There he sang of Hiawatha,
Sang the Song of Hiawatha,
Sang his wondrous birth and being,
How he prayed and how he fasted,
How he lived, and toiled, and suffered,
That the tribes of men might prosper,
That he might advance his people!"

Ye who love the haunts of Nature,

Love the sunshine of the meadow,
Love the shadow of the forest,
Love the wind among the branches,
And the rain-shower and the snow-storm,
And the rushing of great rivers
Through their palisades of pine-trees,
And the thunder in the mountains,
Whose innumerable echoes
Flap like eagles in their eyries; —
Listen to these wild traditions,
To this Song of Hiawatha!

    Ye who love a nation's legends,
Love the ballads of a people,
That like voices from afar off
Call to us to pause and listen,
Speak in tones so plain and childlike,
Scarcely can the ear distinguish
Whether they are sung or spoken; —
Listen to this Indian Legend,
To this Song of Hiawatha!

    Ye whose hearts are fresh and simple,
Who have faith in God and Nature,
Who believe, that in all ages
Every human heart is human,
That in even savage bosoms
There are longings, yearnings, strivings
For the good they comprehend not,

That the feeble hands and helpless,
Groping blindly in the darkness,
Touch God's right hand in that darkness
And are lifted up and strengthened ; —
Listen to this simple story,
To this Song of Hiawatha !

   Ye, who sometimes, in your rambles
Through the green lanes of the country,
Where the tangled barberry-bushes
Hang their tufts of crimson berries
Over stone walls gray with mosses,
Pause by some neglected graveyard,
For a while to muse, and ponder
On a half-effaced inscription,
Written with little skill of song-craft,
Homely phrases, but each letter
Full of hope and yet of heart-break,
Full of all the tender pathos
Of the Here and the Hereafter ; —
Stay and read this rude inscription,
Read this Song of Hiawatha !

The Song of Hiawatha

I

The Peace-Pipe

On the Mountains of the Prairie,
On the great Red Pipe-stone Quarry,
Gitche Manito, the mighty,
He the Master of Life, descending,
On the red crags of the quarry
Stood erect, and called the nations,
Called the tribes of men together.
  From his footprints flowed a river,
Leaped into the light of morning,
O'er the precipice plunging downward

Gleamed like Ishkoodah, the comet.
And the Spirit, stooping earthward,
With his finger on the meadow
Traced a winding pathway for it,
Saying to it, "Run in this way!"

From the red stone of the quarry
With his hand he broke a fragment,
Moulded it into a pipe-head,
Shaped and fashioned it with figures;
From the margin of the river
Took a long reed for a pipe-stem,
With its dark green leaves upon it;
Filled the pipe with bark of willow,
With the bark of the red willow;
Breathed upon the neighboring forest,
Made its great boughs chafe together,
Till in flame they burst and kindled;
And erect upon the mountains,
Gitche Manito, the mighty,
Smoked the calumet, the Peace-Pipe,
As a signal to the nations.

And the smoke rose slowly, slowly,
Through the tranquil air of morning,
First a single line of darkness,
Then a denser, bluer vapor,
Then a snow-white cloud unfolding,
Like the tree-tops of the forest,

Ever rising, rising, rising,
Till it touched the top of heaven,
Till it broke against the heaven,
And rolled outward all around it.

From the Vale of Tawasentha,
From the Valley of Wyoming,
From the groves of Tuscaloosa,
From the far-off Rocky Mountains,
From the Northern lakes and rivers
All the tribes beheld the signal,
Saw the distant smoke ascending,
The Pukwana of the Peace-Pipe.

And the Prophets of the nations
Said: "Behold it, the Pukwana!
By this signal from afar off,
Bending like a wand of willow,
Waving like a hand that beckons,
Gitche Manito, the mighty,
Calls the tribes of men together,
Calls the warriors to his council!"

Down the rivers, o'er the prairies,
Came the warriors of the nations,
Came the Delawares and Mohawks,
Came the Choctaws and Camanches,
Came the Shoshonies and Blackfeet,
Came the Pawnees and Omahas,
Came the Mandans and Dacotahs,

All the tribes beheld the signal,
Saw the distant smoke ascending

Came the Hurons and Ojibways,
All the warriors drawn together
By the signal of the Peace-Pipe,
To the Mountains of the Prairie,
To the great Red Pipe-stone Quarry.

   And they stood there on the meadow,
With their weapons and their war-gear,
Painted like the leaves of Autumn,
Painted like the sky of morning,
Wildly glaring at each other;
In their faces stern defiance,
In their hearts the feuds of ages,
The hereditary hatred,
The ancestral thirst of vengeance.

   Gitche Manito, the mighty,
The creator of the nations,
Looked upon them with compassion,
With paternal love and pity;
Looked upon their wrath and wrangling
But as quarrels among children,
But as feuds and fights of children!

   Over them he stretched his right hand,
To subdue their stubborn natures,
To allay their thirst and fever,
By the shadow of his right hand;
Spake to them with voice majestic
As the sound of far-off waters,

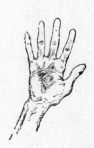

Falling into deep abysses,
Warning, chiding, spake in this wise : —
  "O my children ! my poor children !
Listen to the words of wisdom,
Listen to the words of warning,
From the lips of the Great Spirit,
From the Master of Life, who made you !

  "I have given you lands to hunt in,
I have given you streams to fish in,
I have given you bear and bison,
I have given you roe and reindeer,
I have given you brant and beaver,
Filled the marshes full of wild-fowl,
Filled the rivers full of fishes ;
Why then are you not contented ?
Why then will you hunt each other ?

  "I am weary of your quarrels,
Weary of your wars and bloodshed,
Weary of your prayers for vengeance,
Of your wranglings and dissensions ;
All your strength is in your union,
All your danger is in discord ;
Therefore be at peace henceforward,
And as brothers live together.

  "I will send a Prophet to you,
A Deliverer of the nations,
Who shall guide you and shall teach you,

Who shall toil and suffer with you.
If you listen to his counsels,
You will multiply and prosper;
If his warnings pass unheeded,
You will fade away and perish!
  "Bathe now in the stream before you,
Wash the war-paint from your faces,
Wash the blood-stains from your fingers,
Bury your war-clubs and your weapons,
Break the red stone from this quarry,
Mould and make it into Peace-Pipes,
Take the reeds that grow beside you,
Deck them with your brightest feathers,
Smoke the calumet together,
And as brothers live henceforward!"

  Then upon the ground the warriors
Threw their cloaks and shirts of deer-skin,
Threw their weapons and their war-gear,
Leaped into the rushing river,
Washed the war-paint from their faces.
Clear above them flowed the water,
Clear and limpid from the footprints
Of the Master of Life descending;
Dark below them flowed the water,
Soiled and stained with streaks of crimson,
As if blood were mingled with it!
  From the river came the warriors,

Clean and washed from all their war-paint;
On the banks their clubs they buried,
Buried all their warlike weapons.
Gitche Manito, the mighty,
The Great Spirit, the creator,
Smiled upon his helpless children!
   And in silence all the warriors
Broke the red stone of the quarry,
Smoothed and formed it into Peace-Pipes,
Broke the long reeds by the river,
Decked them with their brightest feathers,
And departed each one homeward,
While the Master of Life, ascending,
Through the opening of cloud-curtains,
Through the doorways of the heaven,
Vanished from before their faces,
In the smoke that rolled around him,
The Pukwana of the Peace-Pipe!

II

The Four Winds

"Honor be to Mudjekeewis!"
Cried the warriors, cried the old men,
When he came in triumph homeward
With the sacred Belt of Wampum,
From the regions of the North-Wind,
From the kingdom of Wabasso,
From the land of the White Rabbit.
    He had stolen the Belt of Wampum
From the neck of Mishe-Mokwa,

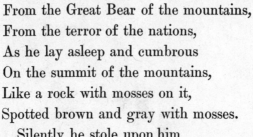

From the Great Bear of the mountains,
From the terror of the nations,
As he lay asleep and cumbrous
On the summit of the mountains,
Like a rock with mosses on it,
Spotted brown and gray with mosses.

Silently he stole upon him
Till the red nails of the monster
Almost touched him, almost scared him,
Till the hot breath of his nostrils
Warmed the hands of Mudjekeewis,
As he drew the Belt of Wampum
Over the round ears, that heard not,
Over the small eyes, that saw not,
Over the long nose and nostrils,
The black muffle of the nostrils,
Out of which the heavy breathing
Warmed the hands of Mudjekeewis.
Then he swung aloft his war-club,
Shouted loud and long his war-cry,
Smote the mighty Mishe-Mokwa
In the middle of the forehead,
Right between the eyes he smote him.

With the heavy blow bewildered,
Rose the Great Bear of the mountains;
But his knees beneath him trembled,
And he whimpered like a woman,

As he reeled and staggered forward,
As he sat upon his haunches;
And the mighty Mudjekeewis,
Standing fearlessly before him,
Taunted him in loud derision,
Spake disdainfully in this wise:—

"Hark you, Bear! you are a coward,
And no Brave, as you pretended;
Else you would not cry and whimper
Like a miserable woman!
Bear! you know our tribes are hostile,
Long have been at war together;
Now you find that we are strongest,
You go sneaking in the forest,
You go hiding in the mountains!
Had you conquered me in battle
Not a groan would I have uttered;
But you, Bear! sit here and whimper,
And disgrace your tribe by crying,
Like a wretched Shaugodaya,
Like a cowardly old woman!"

Then again he raised his war-club,
Smote again the Mishe-Mokwa
In the middle of his forehead,
Broke his skull, as ice is broken
When one goes to fish in Winter.
Thus was slain the Mishe-Mokwa,

He the Great Bear of the mountains,
He the terror of the nations.
    " Honor be to Mudjekeewis ! "
With a shout exclaimed the people,
" Honor be to Mudjekeewis !
Henceforth he shall be the West-Wind,
And hereafter and forever
Shall he hold supreme dominion
Over all the winds of heaven.
Call him no more Mudjekeewis,
Call him Kabeyun, the West-Wind ! "
    Thus was Mudjekeewis chosen
Father of the Winds of Heaven.
For himself he kept the West-Wind,
Gave the others to his children ;
Unto Wabun gave the East-Wind,
Gave the South to Shawondasee,
And the North-Wind, wild and cruel,
To the fierce Kabibonokka.
    Young and beautiful was Wabun ;
He it was who brought the morning,
He it was whose silver arrows
Chased the dark o'er hill and valley ;
He it was whose cheeks were painted
With the brightest streaks of crimson,
And whose voice awoke the village,
Called the deer, and called the hunter.

Lonely in the sky was Wabun;
Though the birds sang gayly to him,
Though the wild-flowers of the meadow
Filled the air with odors for him;
Though the forests and the rivers
Sang and shouted at his coming,
Still his heart was sad within him,
For he was alone in heaven.

But one morning, gazing earthward,
While the village still was sleeping,
And the fog lay on the river,
Like a ghost, that goes at sunrise,
He beheld a maiden walking
All alone upon a meadow,
Gathering water-flags and rushes
By a river in the meadow.

Every morning, gazing earthward,
Still the first thing he beheld there
Was her blue eyes looking at him,
Two blue lakes among the rushes.
And he loved the lonely maiden,
Who thus waited for his coming;
For they both were solitary,
She on earth and he in heaven.

And he wooed her with caresses,
Wooed her with his smile of sunshine,
With his flattering words he wooed her,

With his sighing and his singing,
Gentlest whispers in the branches,
Softest music, sweetest odors,
Till he drew her to his bosom,
Folded in his robes of crimson,
Till into a star he changed her,
Trembling still upon his bosom;
And forever in the heavens
They are seen together walking,
Wabun and the Wabun-Annung,
Wabun and the Star of Morning.

But the fierce Kabibonokka
Had his dwelling among icebergs,
In the everlasting snow-drifts,
In the kingdom of Wabasso,
In the land of the White Rabbit.
He it was whose hand in Autumn
Painted all the trees with scarlet,
Stained the leaves with red and yellow;
He it was who sent the snow-flakes,
Sifting, hissing through the forest,
Froze the ponds, the lakes, the rivers,
Drove the loon and sea-gull southward,
Drove the cormorant and curlew
To their nests of sedge and sea-tang
In the realms of Shawondasee.

Once the fierce Kabibonokka

Like a ghost that goes at sunrise
He beheld a maiden walking

Issued from his lodge of snow-drifts,
From his home among the icebergs,
And his hair, with snow besprinkled,
Streamed behind him like a river,
Like a black and wintry river,
As he howled and hurried southward,
Over frozen lakes and moorlands.

There among the reeds and rushes
Found he Shingebis, the diver,
Trailing strings of fish behind him,
O'er the frozen fens and moorlands,
Lingering still among the moorlands,
Though his tribe had long departed
To the land of Shawondasee.

Cried the fierce Kabibonokka,
" Who is this that dares to brave me ?
Dares to stay in my dominions,
When the Wawa has departed,
When the wild-goose has gone southward,
And the heron, the Shuh-shuh-gah,
Long ago departed southward ?
I will go into his wigwam,
I will put his smouldering fire out ! "

And at night Kabibonokka
To the lodge came wild and wailing,
Heaped the snow in drifts about it,
Shouted down into the smoke-flue,

Shook the lodge-poles in his fury,
Flapped the curtain of the doorway.
Shingebis, the diver, feared not,
Shingebis, the diver, cared not;
Four great logs had he for firewood,
One for each moon of the winter,
And for food the fishes served him.
By his blazing fire he sat there,
Warm and merry, eating, laughing,
Singing, " O Kabibonokka,
You are but my fellow-mortal ! "
    Then Kabibonokka entered,
And though Shingebis, the diver,
Felt his presence by the coldness,
Felt his icy breath upon him,
Still he did not cease his singing,
Still he did not leave his laughing,
Only turned the log a little,
Only made the fire burn brighter,
Made the sparks fly up the smoke-flue.
    From Kabibonokka's forehead,
From his snow-besprinkled tresses,
Drops of sweat fell fast and heavy,
Making dints upon the ashes,
As along the eaves of lodges,
As from drooping boughs of hemlock,
Drips the melting snow in spring-time,
Making hollows in the snow-drifts.

Till at last he rose defeated,
Could not bear the heat and laughter,
Could not bear the merry singing,
But rushed headlong through the doorway,
Stamped upon the crusted snow-drifts,
Stamped upon the lakes and rivers,
Made the snow upon them harder,
Made the ice upon them thicker,
Challenged Shingebis, the diver,
To come forth and wrestle with him,
To come forth and wrestle naked
On the frozen fens and moorlands.

Forth went Shingebis, the diver,
Wrestled all night with the North-Wind,
Wrestled naked on the moorlands
With the fierce Kabibonokka,
Till his panting breath grew fainter,
Till his frozen grasp grew feebler,
Till he reeled and staggered backward,
And retreated, baffled, beaten,
To the kingdom of Wabasso,
To the land of the White Rabbit,
Hearing still the gusty laughter,
Hearing Shingebis, the diver,
Singing, " O Kabibonokka,
You are but my fellow-mortal ! "

Shawondasee, fat and lazy,
Had his dwelling far to southward,

In the drowsy, dreamy sunshine,
In the never-ending Summer.
He it was who sent the wood-birds,
Sent the robin, the Opechee,
Sent the blue-bird, the Owaissa,
Sent the Shawshaw, sent the swallow,
Sent the wild-goose, Wawa, northward,
Sent the melons and tobacco,
And the grapes in purple clusters.

From his pipe the smoke ascending
Filled the sky with haze and vapor,
Filled the air with dreamy softness,
Gave a twinkle to the water,
Touched the rugged hills with smoothness,
Brought the tender Indian Summer
To the melancholy North-land,
In the dreary Moon of Snow-shoes.

Listless, careless Shawondasee!
In his life he had one shadow,
In his heart one sorrow had he.
Once, as he was gazing northward,
Far away upon a prairie
He beheld a maiden standing,
Saw a tall and slender maiden
All alone upon a prairie ;
Brightest green were all her garments,
And her hair was like the sunshine.

Day by day he gazed upon her,
Day by day he sighed with passion,
Day by day his heart within him
Grew more hot with love and longing
For the maid with yellow tresses.
But he was too fat and lazy
To bestir himself and woo her.
Yes, too indolent and easy
To pursue her and persuade her ;
So he only gazed upon her,
Only sat and sighed with passion
For the maiden of the prairie.

Till one morning, looking northward,
He beheld her yellow tresses
Changed and covered o'er with whiteness,
Covered as with whitest snow-flakes.
" Ah ! my brother from the North-land,
From the kingdom of Wabasso,
From the land of the White Rabbit !
You have stolen the maiden from me,
You have laid your hand upon her,
You have wooed and won my maiden,
With your stories of the North-land ! "
Thus the wretched Shawondasee
Breathed into the air his sorrow ;
And the South-Wind o'er the prairie
Wandered warm with sighs of passion,

With the sighs of Shawondasee,
Till the air seemed full of snow-flakes,
Full of thistle-down the prairie,
And the maid with hair like sunshine
Vanished from his sight forever ;
Never more did Shawondaseee
See the maid with yellow tresses !

    Poor, deluded Shawondasee !
'T was no woman that you gazed at,
'T was no maiden that you sighed for,
'T was the prairie dandelion
That through all the dreamy Summer
You had gazed at with such longing,
You had sighed for with such passion,
And had puffed away forever,
Blown into the air with sighing.
Ah ! deluded Shawondasee !

    Thus the Four Winds were divided ;
Thus the sons of Mudjekeewis
Had their stations in the heavens,
At the corners of the heavens ;
For himself the West-Wind only
Kept the mighty Mudjekeewis.

III

Hiawatha's Childhood

Downward through the evening twilight,
In the days that are forgotten,
In the unremembered ages,
From the full moon fell Nokomis,
Fell the beautiful Nokomis,
She a wife, but not a mother.

  She was sporting with her women,
Swinging in a swing of grape-vines,
When her rival the rejected,
Full of jealousy and hatred,
Cut the leafy swing asunder,
Cut in twain the twisted grape-vines,
And Nokomis fell affrighted
Downward through the evening twilight,
On the Muskoday, the meadow,

On the prairie full of blossoms.
"See! a star falls!" said the people;
"From the sky a star is falling!"

There among the ferns and mosses,
There among the prairie lilies,
On the Muskoday, the meadow,
In the moonlight and the starlight,
Fair Nokomis bore a daughter.
And she called her name Wenonah,
As the first-born of her daughters.
And the daughter of Nokomis
Grew up like the prairie lilies,
Grew a tall and slender maiden,
With the beauty of the moonlight,
With the beauty of the starlight.

And Nokomis warned her often,
Saying oft, and oft repeating,
"Oh, beware of Mudjekeewis,
Of the West-Wind, Mudjekeewis;
Listen not to what he tells you;
Lie not down upon the meadow,
Stoop not down among the lilies,
Lest the West-Wind come and harm you!"

But she heeded not the warning,
Heeded not those words of wisdom,
And the West-Wind came at evening,
Walking lightly o'er the prairie,

Whispering to the leaves and blossoms,
Bending low the flowers and grasses,
Found the beautiful Wenonah,
Lying there among the lilies,
Wooed her with his words of sweetness,
Wooed her with his soft caresses,
Till she bore a son in sorrow,
Bore a son of love and sorrow.

Thus was born my Hiawatha,
Thus was born the child of wonder;
But the daughter of Nokomis,
Hiawatha's gentle mother,
In her anguish died deserted
By the West-Wind, false and faithless,
By the heartless Mudjekeewis.

For her daughter long and loudly
Wailed and wept the sad Nokomis;
" Oh that I were dead ! " she murmured,
" Oh that I were dead, as thou art !
No more work, and no more weeping,
Wahonowin ! Wahonowin ! "

By the shores of Gitche Gumee,
By the shining Big-Sea-Water,
Stood the wigwam of Nokomis,
Daughter of the Moon, Nokomis.
Dark behind it rose the forest,
Rose the black and gloomy pine-trees,

Rose the firs with cones upon them;
Bright before it beat the water,
Beat the clear and sunny water,
Beat the shining Big-Sea-Water.
    There the wrinkled old Nokomis
Nursed the little Hiawatha,
Rocked him in his linden cradle,
Bedded soft in moss and rushes,
Safely bound with reindeer sinews;
Stilled his fretful wail by saying,
" Hush! the Naked Bear will hear thee! "
Lulled him into slumber, singing,
" Ewa-yea! my little owlet!
Who is this, that lights the wigwam?
With his great eyes lights the wigwam?
Ewa-yea! my little owlet! "
    Many things Nokomis taught him
Of the stars that shine in heaven;
Showed him Ishkoodah, the comet,
Ishkoodah, with fiery tresses;
Showed the Death-Dance of the spirits,
Warriors with their plumes and war-clubs,
Flaring far away to northward
In the frosty nights of Winter;
Showed the broad white road in heaven,
Pathway of the ghosts, the shadows,

Running straight across the heavens,
Crowded with the ghosts, the shadows.

At the door on summer evenings
Sat the little Hiawatha;
Heard the whispering of the pine-trees,
Heard the lapping of the waters,
Sounds of music, words of wonder;
"Minne-wawa!" said the pine-trees,
"Mudway-aushka!" said the water.

Saw the fire-fly, Wah-wah-taysee,
Flitting through the dusk of evening,
With the twinkle of its candle
Lighting up the brakes and bushes,
And he sang the song of children,
Sang the song Nokomis taught him:
"Wah-wah-taysee, little fire-fly,
Little, flitting, white-fire insect,
Little, dancing, white-fire creature,
Light me with your little candle,
Ere upon my bed I lay me,
Ere in sleep I close my eyelids!"

Saw the moon rise from the water
Rippling, rounding from the water,
Saw the flecks and shadows on it,
Whispered, "What is that, Nokomis?"
And the good Nokomis answered:

" Once a warrior, very angry,
Seized his grandmother, and threw her
Up into the sky at midnight ;
Right against the moon he threw her ;
'T is her body that you see there."

Saw the rainbow in the heaven,
In the eastern sky, the rainbow,
Whispered, " What is that, Nokomis ? "
And the good Nokomis answered :

" 'T is the heaven of flowers you see there ;
All the wild-flowers of the forest,
All the lilies of the prairie,
When on earth they fade and perish,
Blossom in that heaven above us."

When he heard the owls at midnight,
Hooting, laughing in the forest,
" What is that ? " he cried in terror,
" What is that ? " he said, " Nokomis ? "
And the good Nokomis answered :
" That is but the owl and owlet,
Talking in their native language,
Talking, scolding at each other."

Then the little Hiawatha
Learned of every bird its language,
Learned their names and all their secrets,
How they built their nests in Summer,
Where they hid themselves in Winter,

Talked with them whene'er he met them,
Called them " Hiawatha's Chickens."
  Of all beasts he learned the language,
Learned their names and all their secrets,
How the beavers built their lodges,
Where the squirrels hid their acorns,
How the reindeer ran so swiftly,
Why the rabbit was so timid,
Talked with them whene'er he met them,
Called them " Hiawatha's Brothers."
  Then Iagoo, the great boaster,
He the marvellous story-teller,
He the traveller and the talker,
He the friend of old Nokomis,
Made a bow for Hiawatha;
From a branch of ash he made it,
From an oak-bough made the arrows,
Tipped with flint, and winged with feathers,
And the cord he made of deer-skin.
  Then he said to Hiawatha:
" Go, my son, into the forest,
Where the red deer herd together,
Kill for us a famous roebuck,
Kill for us a deer with antlers ! "
  Forth into the forest straightway
All alone walked Hiawatha
Proudly, with his bow and arrows;

And the birds sang round him, o'er him,
" Do not shoot us, Hiawatha! "
Sang the robin, the Opechee,
Sang the bluebird, the Owaissa,
" Do not shoot us, Hiawatha! "
    Up the oak-tree, close beside him,
Sprang the squirrel, Adjidaumo,
In and out among the branches,
Coughed and chattered from the oak-tree,
Laughed, and said between his laughing,
" Do not shoot me, Hiawatha! "
    And the rabbit from his pathway
Leaped aside, and at a distance
Sat erect upon his haunches,
Half in fear and half in frolic,
Saying to the little hunter,
" Do not shoot me, Hiawatha! "
    But he heeded not, nor heard them,
For his thoughts were with the red deer ;
On their tracks his eyes were fastened,
Leading downward to the river,
To the ford across the river,
And as one in slumber walked he.
    Hidden in the alder-bushes,
There he waited till the deer came,
Till he saw two antlers lifted,
Saw two eyes look from the thicket,

Then, upon one knee uprising,
Hiawatha aimed an arrow

Saw two nostrils point to windward,
And a deer came down the pathway,
Flecked with leafy light and shadow.
And his heart within him fluttered,
Trembled like the leaves above him,
Like the birch-leaf palpitated,
As the deer came down the pathway.

Then, upon one knee uprising,
Hiawatha aimed an arrow;
Scarce a twig moved with his motion,
Scarce a leaf was stirred or rustled,
But the wary roebuck started,
Stamped with all his hoofs together,
Listened with one foot uplifted,
Leaped as if to meet the arrow;
Ah! the singing, fatal arrow,
Like a wasp it buzzed and stung him!

Dead he lay there in the forest,
By the ford across the river;
Beat his timid heart no longer,
But the heart of Hiawatha

Throbbed and shouted and exulted,
As he bore the red deer homeward,
And Iagoo and Nokomis
Hailed his coming with applauses.

From the red deer's hide Nokomis
Make a cloak for Hiawatha,

From the red deer's flesh Nokomis
Made a banquet to his honor.
All the village came and feasted,
All the guests praised Hiawatha,
Called him Strong-Heart, Soan-ge-taha !
Called him Loon-Heart, Mahn-go-taysee !

IV

Hiawatha and Mudjekeewis

Out of childhood into manhood
Now had grown my Hiawatha,
Skilled in all the craft of hunters,
Learned in all the lore of old men,
In all youthful sports and pastimes,
In all manly arts and labors.

Swift of foot was Hiawatha;

He could shoot an arrow from him,
And run forward with such fleetness,
That the arrow fell behind him!
Strong of arm was Hiawatha;
He could shoot ten arrows upward,
Shoot them with such strength and swiftness,
That the tenth had left the bow-string
Ere the first to earth had fallen!

He had mittens, Minjekahwun,
Magic mittens made of deer-skin;
When upon his hands he wore them,
He could smite the rocks asunder,
He could grind them into powder.
He had moccasins enchanted,
Magic moccasins of deer-skin;
When he bound them round his ankles,
When upon his feet he tied them,
At each stride a mile he measured!

Much he questioned old Nokomis
Of his father Mudjekeewis;
Learned from her the fatal secret
Of the beauty of his mother,
Of the falsehood of his father;
And his heart was hot within him,
Like a living coal his heart was.

Then he said to old Nokomis,
"I will go to Mudjekeewis,

See how fares it with my father,
At the doorways of the West-Wind,
At the portals of the Sunset!"
From his lodge went Hiawatha,
Dressed for travel, armed for hunting;
Dressed in deer-skin shirt and leggings,
Richly wrought with quills and wampum;
On his head his eagle-feathers,
Round his waist his belt of wampum,
In his hand his bow of ash-wood,
Strung with sinews of the reindeer;
In his quiver oaken arrows,
Tipped with jasper, winged with feathers;
With his mittens, Minjekahwun,
With his moccasins enchanted.

Warning said the old Nokomis,
"Go not forth, O Hiawatha!
To the kingdom of the West-Wind,
To the realms of Mudjekeewis,
Lest he harm you with his magic,
Lest he kill you with his cunning!"
But the fearless Hiawatha
Heeded not her woman's warning;
Forth he strode into the forest,
At each stride a mile he measured;
Lurid seemed the sky above him,
Lurid seemed the earth beneath him,

Hot and close the air around him,
Filled with smoke and fiery vapors,
As of burning woods and prairies,
For his heart was hot within him,
Like a living coal his heart was.

So he journeyed westward, westward,
Left the fleetest deer behind him,
Left the antelope and bison ;
Crossed the rushing Esconaba,
Crossed the mighty Mississippi,
Passed the Mountains of the Prairie,
Passed the land of Crows and Foxes,
Passed the dwellings of the Blackfeet,
Came unto the Rocky Mountains,
To the kingdom of the West-Wind,
Where upon the gusty summits
Sat the ancient Mudjekeewis,
Ruler of the winds of heaven.

Filled with awe was Hiawatha
At the aspect of his father.
On the air about him wildly
Tossed and streamed his cloudy tresses,
Gleamed like drifting snow his tresses,
Glared like Ishkoodah, the comet,
Like the star with fiery tresses.

Filled with joy was Mudjekeewis
When he looked on Hiawatha,

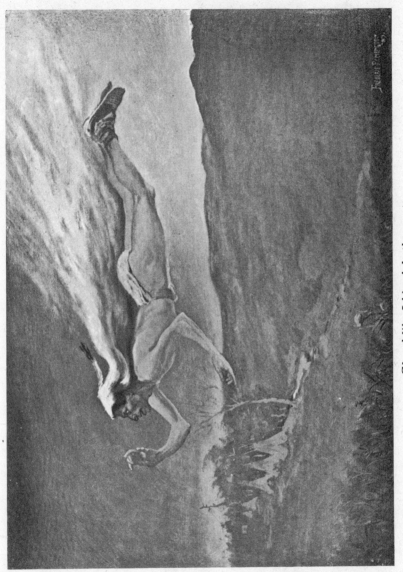

Glared like Ishkoodah, the comet,
Like the star with fiery tresses

Saw his youth rise up before him
In the face of Hiawatha,
Saw the beauty of Wenonah
From the grave rise up before him.

 " Welcome ! " said he, " Hiawatha,
To the kingdom of the West-Wind !
Long have I been waiting for you !
Youth is lovely, age is lonely,
Youth is fiery, age is frosty ;
You bring back the days departed,
You bring back my youth of passion,
And the beautiful Wenonah ! "

 Many days they talked together,
Questioned, listened, waited, answered ;
Much the mighty Mudjekeewis
Boasted of his ancient prowess,
Of his perilous adventures,
His indomitable courage,
His invulnerable body.

 Patiently sat Hiawatha,
Listening to his father's boasting ;
With a smile he sat and listened,
Uttered neither threat nor menace,
Neither word nor look betrayed him,
But his heart was hot within him,
Like a living coal his heart was.

 Then he said, " O Mudjekeewis,

Is there nothing that can harm you?
Nothing that you are afraid of?"
And the mighty Mudjekeewis,
Grand and gracious in his boasting,
Answered, saying, "There is nothing,
Nothing but the black rock yonder,
Nothing but the fatal Wawbeek!"

And he looked at Hiawatha
With a wise look and benignant,
With a countenance paternal,
Looked with pride upon the beauty
Of his tall and graceful figure,
Saying, "O my Hiawatha!
Is there anything can harm you?
Anything you are afraid of?"

But the wary Hiawatha
Paused awhile, as if uncertain,
Held his peace, as if resolving,
And then answered, "There is nothing,
Nothing but the bulrush yonder,
Nothing but the great Apukwa!"

And as Mudjekeewis, rising,
Stretched his hand to pluck the bulrush,
Hiawatha cried in terror,
Cried in well-dissembled terror,
"Kago! kago! do not touch it!"
"Ah, kaween!" said Mudjekeewis,
"No indeed, I will not touch it!"

Then they talked of other matters;
First of Hiawatha's brothers,
First of Wabun, of the East-Wind,
Of the South-Wind, Shawondasee,
Of the North, Kabibonokka;
Then of Hiawatha's mother,
Of the beautiful Wenonah,
Of her birth upon the meadow,
Of her death, as old Nokomis
Had remembered and related.

And he cried, " O Mudjekeewis,
It was you who killed Wenonah,
Took her young life and her beauty,
Broke the Lily of the Prairie,
Trampled it beneath your footsteps;
You confess it! you confess it!"
And the mighty Mudjekeewis
Tossed upon the wind his tresses,
Bowed his hoary head in anguish,
With a silent nod assented.

Then up started Hiawatha,
And with threatening look and gesture
Laid his hand upon the black rock,
On the fatal Wawbeek laid it,
With his mittens, Minjekahwun,
Rent the jutting crag asunder,
Smote and crushed it into fragments,
Hurled them madly at his father,

The remorseful Mudjekeewis,
For his heart was hot within him,
Like a living coal his heart was.

    But the ruler of the West-Wind
Blew the fragments backward from him,
With the breathing of his nostrils,
With the tempest of his anger,
Blew them back at his assailant;
Seized the bulrush, the Apukwa,
Dragged it with its roots and fibres
From the margin of the meadow,
From its ooze the giant bulrush;
Long and loud laughed Hiawatha!

    Then began the deadly conflict,
Hand to hand among the mountains;
From his eyry screamed the eagle,
The Keneu, the great war-eagle,
Sat upon the crags around them,
Wheeling flapped his wings above them.

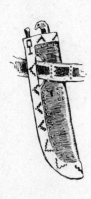

    Like a tall tree in the tempest
Bent and lashed the giant bulrush;
And in masses huge and heavy
Crashing fell the fatal Wawbeek;
Till the earth shook with the tumult
And confusion of the battle,
And the air was full of shoutings,
And the thunder of the mountains,
Starting, answered, " Baim-wawa ! "

Back retreated Mudjekeewis,
Rushing westward o'er the mountains,
Stumbling westward down the mountains,
Three whole days retreated fighting,
Still pursued by Hiawatha
To the doorways of the West-Wind,
To the portals of the Sunset,
To the earth's remotest border,
Where into the empty spaces
Sinks the sun, as a flamingo
Drops into her nest at nightfall
In the melancholy marshes.

"Hold!" at length cried Mudjekeewis,
"Hold, my son, my Hiawatha!
'T is impossible to kill me,
For you cannot kill the immortal.
I have put you to this trial,
But to know and prove your courage;
Now receive the prize of valor!

"Go back to your home and people,
Live among them, toil among them,
Cleanse the earth from all that harms it,
Clear the fishing-grounds and rivers,
Slay all monsters and magicians,
All the Wendigoes, the giants,
All the serpents, the Kenabeeks,
As I slew the Mishe-Mokwa,
Slew the Great Bear of the mountains.

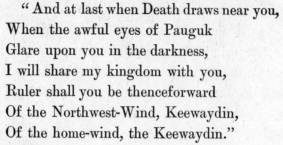

"And at last when Death draws near you,
When the awful eyes of Pauguk
Glare upon you in the darkness,
I will share my kingdom with you,
Ruler shall you be thenceforward
Of the Northwest-Wind, Keewaydin,
Of the home-wind, the Keewaydin."

Thus was fought that famous battle
In the dreadful days of Shah-shah,
In the days long since departed,
In the kingdom of the West-Wind.
Still the hunter sees its traces
Scattered far o'er hill and valley;
Sees the giant bulrush growing
By the ponds and water-courses,
Sees the masses of the Wawbeek
Lying still in every valley.

Homeward now went Hiawatha;
Pleasant was the landscape round him,
Pleasant was the air above him,
For the bitterness of anger
Had departed wholly from him,
From his brain the thought of vengeance,
From his heart the burning fever.

Only once his pace he slackened,
Only once he paused or halted,
Paused to purchase heads of arrows

Of the ancient Arrow-maker,
In the land of the Dacotahs,
Where the Falls of Minnehaha
Flash and gleam among the oak-trees,
Laugh and leap into the valley.

There the ancient Arrow-maker
Made his arrow-heads of sandstone,
Arrow-heads of chalcedony,
Arrow-heads of flint and jasper,
Smoothed and sharpened at the edges,
Hard and polished, keen and costly.

With him dwelt his dark-eyed daughter,
Wayward as the Minnehaha,
With her moods of shade and sunshine,
Eyes that smiled and frowned alternate,
Feet as rapid as the river,
Tresses flowing like the water,
And as musical a laughter :
And he named her from the river,
From the water-fall he named her,
Minnehaha, Laughing Water.

Was it then for heads of arrows,
Arrow-heads of chalcedony,
Arrow-heads of flint and jasper,
That my Hiawatha halted
In the land of the Dacotahs?

Was it not to see the maiden,

See the face of Laughing Water
Peeping from behind the curtain,
Hear the rustling of her garments
From behind the waving curtain,
As one sees the Minnehaha
Gleaming, glancing through the branches,
As one hears the Laughing Water
From behind its screen of branches?
    Who shall say what thoughts and visions
Fill the fiery brains of young men?
Who shall say what dreams of beauty
Filled the heart of Hiawatha?
All he told to old Nokomis,
When he reached the lodge at sunset,
Was the meeting with his father,
Was his fight with Mudjekeewis;
Not a word he said of arrows,
Not a word of Laughing Water.

V

Hiawatha's Fasting

You shall hear how Hiawatha
Prayed and fasted in the forest,
Not for greater skill in hunting,
Not for greater craft in fishing,
Not for triumphs in the battle,

And renown among the warriors,
But for profit of the people,
For advantage of the nations.

First he built a lodge for fasting,
Built a wigwam in the forest,
By the shining Big-Sea-Water,
In the blithe and pleasant Spring-time,
In the Moon of Leaves he built it,
And, with dreams and visions many,
Seven whole days and nights he fasted.

On the first day of his fasting
Through the leafy woods he wandered;
Saw the deer start from the thicket,
Saw the rabbit in his burrow,
Heard the pheasant, Bena, drumming,
Heard the squirrel, Adjidaumo,
Rattling in his hoard of acorns,
Saw the pigeon, the Omeme,
Building nests among the pine-trees,
And in flocks the wild goose, Wawa,
Flying to the fen-lands northward,
Whirring, wailing far above him.

" Master of Life ! " he cried, desponding,
" Must our lives depend on these things ? "

On the next day of his fasting
By the river's brink he wandered,
Through the Muskoday, the meadow,

Saw the wild rice, Mahnomonee,
Saw the blueberry, Meenahga,
And the strawberry, Odahmin,
And the gooseberry, Shahbomin,
And the grape-vine, the Bemahgut,
Trailing o'er the alder-branches,
Filling all the air with fragrance !
"Master of Life !" he cried, desponding,
"Must our lives depend on these things ?"
 On the third day of his fasting
By the lake he sat and pondered,
By the still, transparent water ;
Saw the sturgeon, Nahma, leaping,
Scattering drops like beads of wampum,
Saw the yellow perch, the Sahwa,
Like a sunbeam in the water,
Saw the pike, the Maskenozha,
And the herring, Okahahwis,
And the Shawgashee, the craw-fish !
"Master of Life !" he cried, desponding,
"Must our lives depend on these things ?"
 On the fourth day of his fasting
In his lodge he lay exhausted ;
From his couch of leaves and branches
Gazing with half-open eyelids,
Full of shadowy dreams and visions,
On the dizzy, swimming landscape,

On the gleaming of the water,
On the splendor of the sunset.

And he saw a youth approaching,
Dressed in garments green and yellow
Coming through the purple twilight,
Through the splendor of the sunset;
Plumes of green bent o'er his forehead,
And his hair was soft and golden.

Standing at the open doorway,
Long he looked at Hiawatha,
Looked with pity and compassion
On his wasted form and features,
And, in accents like the sighing
Of the South-Wind in the tree-tops,
Said he, " O my Hiawatha!
All your prayers are heard in heaven,
For you pray not like the others;
Not for greater skill in hunting,
Not for greater craft in fishing,
Not for triumph in the battle,
Nor renown among the warriors,
But for profit of the people,
For advantage of the nations.

" From the Master of Life descending,
I, the friend of man, Mondamin,
Come to warn you and instruct you,
How by struggle and by labor

And he saw a youth approaching,
Dressed in garments green and yellow

You shall gain what you have prayed for.
Rise up from your bed of branches,
Rise, O youth, and wrestle with me!"
　　Faint with famine, Hiawatha
Started from his bed of branches,
From the twilight of his wigwam
Forth into the flush of sunset
Came, and wrestled with Mondamin;
At his touch he felt new courage
Throbbing in his brain and bosom,
Felt new life and hope and vigor
Run through every nerve and fibre.
　　So they wrestled there together
In the glory of the sunset,
And the more they strove and struggled,
Stronger still grew Hiawatha;
Till the darkness fell around them,
And the heron, the Shuh-shuh-gah,
From her nest among the pine-trees,
Gave a cry of lamentation,
Gave a scream of pain and famine.
　　" 'T is enough!" then said Mondamin,
Smiling upon Hiawatha,
" But to-morrow, when the sun sets,
I will come again to try you."
And he vanished, and was seen not;
Whether sinking as the rain sinks,

Whether rising as the mists rise,
Hiawatha saw not, knew not,
Only saw that he had vanished,
Leaving him alone and fainting,
With the misty lake below him,
And the reeling stars above him.

On the morrow and the next day,
When the sun through heaven descending,
Like a red and burning cinder
From the hearth of the Great Spirit,
Fell into the western waters,
Came Mondamin for the trial,
For the strife with Hiawatha;
Came as silent as the dew comes,
From the empty air appearing,
Into empty air returning,
Taking shape when earth it touches,
But invisible to all men
In its coming and its going.

Thrice they wrestled there together
In the glory of the sunset,
Till the darkness fell around them,
Till the heron, the Shuh-shuh-gah,
From her nest among the pine-trees,
Uttered her loud cry of famine,
And Mondamin paused to listen.

Tall and beautiful he stood there,

To and fro his plumes above him
Waved and nodded with his breathing,
And the sweat of the encounter
Stood like drops of dew upon him.

And he cried, " O Hiawatha !
Bravely have you wrestled with me,
Thrice have wrestled stoutly with me,
And the Master of Life, who sees us,
He will give to you the triumph ! "

Then he smiled, and said : " To-morrow
Is the last day of your conflict,
Is the last day of your fasting.
You will conquer and o'ercome me ;
Make a bed for me to lie in,
Where the rain may fall upon me,
Where the sun may come and warm me ;
Strip these garments, green and yellow,
Strip this nodding plumage from me,
Lay me in the earth, and make it
Soft and loose and light above me.

" Let no hand disturb my slumber,
Let no weed nor worm molest me,
Let not Kahgahgee, the raven,
Come to haunt me and molest me,
Only come yourself to watch me,
Till I wake, and start, and quicken,
Till I leap into the sunshine."

And thus saying, he departed ;

Peacefully slept Hiawatha,
But he heard the Wawonaissa,
Heard the whippoorwill complaining,
Perched upon his lonely wigwam;
Heard the rushing Sebowisha,
Heard the rivulet rippling near him,
Talking to the darksome forest;
Heard the sighing of the branches,
As they lifted and subsided
At the passing of the night-wind,
Heard them, as one hears in slumber
Far-off murmurs, dreamy whispers:
Peacefully slept Hiawatha.

On the morrow came Nokomis,
On the seventh day of his fasting,
Came with food for Hiawatha,
Came imploring and bewailing,
Lest his hunger should o'ercome him,
Lest his fasting should be fatal.

But he tasted not, and touched not,
Only said to her, " Nokomis,
Wait until the sun is setting,
Till the darkness falls around us,
Till the heron, the Shuh-shuh-gah,
Crying from the desolate marshes,
Tells us that the day is ended."

Homeward weeping went Nokomis,

Sorrowing for her Hiawatha,
Fearing lest his strength should fail him,
Lest his fasting should be fatal.
He meanwhile sat weary waiting
For the coming of Mondamin,
Till the shadows, pointing eastward,
Lengthened over field and forest,
Till the sun dropped from the heaven,
Floating on the waters westward,
As a red leaf in the Autumn
Falls and floats upon the water,
Falls and sinks into its bosom.

   And behold! the young Mondamin,
With his soft and shining tresses,
With his garments green and yellow,
With his long and glossy plumage,
Stood and beckoned at the doorway,
And as one in slumber walking,
Pale and haggard, but undaunted,
From the wigwam Hiawatha
Came and wrestled with Mondamin.

   Round about him spun the landscape,
Sky and forest reeled together,
And his strong heart leaped within him,
As the sturgeon leaps and struggles
In a net to break its meshes.
Like a ring of fire around him

Blazed and flared the red horizon,
And a hundred suns seemed looking
At the combat of the wrestlers.
    Suddenly upon the greensward
All alone stood Hiawatha,
Panting with his wild exertion,
Palpitating with the struggle;
And before him breathless, lifeless,
Lay the youth, with hair dishevelled,
Plumage torn, and garments tattered,
Dead he lay there in the sunset.
    And victorious Hiawatha
Made the grave as he commanded,
Stripped the garments from Mondamin,
Stripped his tattered plumage from him,
Laid him in the earth, and made it
Soft and loose and light above him;
And the heron, the Shuh-shuh-gah,
From the melancholy moorlands,
Gave a cry of lamentation,
Gave a cry of pain and anguish!
    Homeward then went Hiawatha
To the lodge of old Nokomis,
And the seven days of his fasting
Were accomplished and completed.
But the place was not forgotten
Where he wrestled with Mondamin;
Nor forgotten nor neglected

Was the grave where lay Mondamin,
Sleeping in the rain and sunshine,
Where his scattered plumes and garments
Faded in the rain and sunshine.

Day by day did Hiawatha
Go to wait and watch beside it;
Kept the dark mould soft above it,
Kept it clean from weeds and insects,
Drove away, with scoffs and shoutings,
Kahgahgee, the king of ravens.

Till at length a small green feather
From the earth shot slowly upward,
Then another and another,
And before the Summer ended
Stood the maize in all its beauty,
With its shining robes about it,
And its long, soft, yellow tresses;
And in rapture Hiawatha
Cried aloud, "It is Mondamin!
Yes, the friend of man, Mondamin!"

Then he called to old Nokomis
And Iagoo, the great boaster,
Showed them where the maize was growing,
Told them of his wondrous vision,
Of his wrestling and his triumph,
Of this new gift to the nations,
Which should be their food forever.

And still later, when the Autumn

Changed the long, green leaves to yellow,
And the soft and juicy kernels
Grew like wampum hard and yellow,
Then the ripened ears he gathered,
Stripped the withered husks from off them,
As he once had stripped the wrestler,
Gave the first Feast of Mondamin,
And made known unto the people
This new gift of the Great Spirit.

VI

Hiawatha's Friends

Two good friends had Hiawatha,
Singled out from all the others,
Bound to him in closest union,
And to whom he gave the right hand
Of his heart, in joy and sorrow;
Chibiabos, the musician,
And the very strong man, Kwasind.
    Straight between them ran the pathway,
Never grew the grass upon it;

Singing birds, that utter falsehoods,
Story-tellers, mischief-makers,
Found no eager ear to listen,
Could not breed ill-will between them,
For they kept each other's counsel,
Spake with naked hearts together,
Pondering much and much contriving
How the tribes of men might prosper.

Most beloved by Hiawatha
Was the gentle Chibiabos,
He the best of all musicians,
He the sweetest of all singers.
Beautiful and childlike was he,
Brave as man is, soft as woman,
Pliant as a wand of willow,
Stately as a deer with antlers.

When he sang, the village listened ;
All the warriors gathered round him,
All the women came to hear him ;
Now he stirred their souls to passion,
Now he melted them to pity.

From the hollow reeds he fashioned
Flutes so musical and mellow,
That the brook, the Sebowisha,
Ceased to murmur in the woodland,
That the wood-birds ceased from singing,
And the squirrel, Adjidaumo,

Ceased his chatter in the oak-tree,
And the rabbit, the Wabasso,
Sat upright to look and listen.

Yes, the brook, the Sebowisha,
Pausing, said, " O Chibiabos,
Teach my waves to flow in music,
Softly as your words in singing ! "
Yes, the bluebird, the Owaissa,
Envious, said, " O Chibiabos,
Teach me tones as wild and wayward,
Teach me songs as full of frenzy ! "
Yes, the robin, the Opechee,
Joyous, said, " O Chibiabos,
Teach me tones as sweet and tender,
Teach me songs as full of gladness ! "
And the whippoorwill, Wawonaissa,
Sobbing, said, " O Chibiabos,
Teach me tones as melancholy,
Teach me songs as full of sadness ! "

All the many sounds of nature
Borrowed sweetness from his singing ;
All the hearts of men were softened
By the pathos of his music ;
For he sang of peace and freedom,
Sang of beauty, love, and longing ;
Sang of death, and life undying
In the Islands of the Blessed,

In the kingdom of Ponemah,
In the land of the Hereafter.
    Very dear to Hiawatha
Was the gentle Chibiabos,
He the best of all musicians,
He the sweetest of all singers ;
For his gentleness he loved him,
And the magic of his singing.
    Dear, too, unto Hiawatha
Was the very strong man, Kwasind,
He the strongest of all mortals,
He the mightiest among many ;
For his very strength he loved him,
For his strength allied to goodness.
    Idle in his youth was Kwasind,
Very listless, dull, and dreamy,
Never played with other children,
Never fished and never hunted,
Not like other children was he ;
But they saw that much he fasted,
Much his Manito entreated,
Much besought his Guardian Spirit.
    "Lazy Kwasind !" said his mother,
"In my work you never help me !
In the Summer you are roaming
Idly in the fields and forest ;
In the Winter you are cowering

O'er the firebrands in the wigwam!
In the coldest days of Winter
I must break the ice for fishing;
With my nets you never help me!
At the door my nets are hanging,
Dripping, freezing with the water;
Go and wring them, Yenadizze!
Go and dry them in the sunshine!"

Slowly, from the ashes, Kwasind
Rose, but made no angry answer;
From the lodge went forth in silence,
Took the nets, that hung together,
Dripping, freezing at the doorway,
Like a wisp of straw he wrung them,
Like a wisp of straw he broke them,
Could not wring them without breaking,
Such the strength was in his fingers.

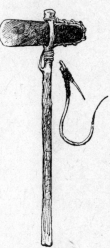

"Lazy Kwasind!" said his father,
"In the hunt you never help me;
Every bow you touch is broken,
Snapped asunder every arrow;
Yet come with me to the forest,
You shall bring the hunting homeward."

Down a narrow pass they wandered,
Where a brooklet led them onward,
Where the trail of deer and bison
Marked the soft mud on the margin,

Till they found all further passage
Shut against them, barred securely
By the trunks of trees uprooted,
Lying lengthwise, lying crosswise,
And forbidding further passage.

" We must go back," said the old man,
" O'er these logs we cannot clamber ;
Not a woodchuck could get through them,
Not a squirrel clamber o'er them ! "
And straightway his pipe he lighted,
And sat down to smoke and ponder.
But before his pipe was finished,
Lo ! the path was cleared before him ;
All the trunks had Kwasind lifted,
To the right hand, to the left hand,
Shot the pine-trees swift as arrows,
Hurled the cedars light as lances.

" Lazy Kwasind ! " said the young men,
As they sported in the meadow :
" Why stand idly looking at us,
Leaning on the rock behind you ?
Come and wrestle with the others,
Let us pitch the quoit together ! "

Lazy Kwasind made no answer,
To their challenge made no answer,
Only rose, and slowly turning,
Seized the huge rock in his fingers,

Pitched it sheer into the river . . .

Where it still is seen in Summer

Tore it from its deep foundation,
Poised it in the air a moment,
Pitched it sheer into the river,
Sheer into the swift Pauwating,
Where it still is seen in Summer.

Once as down that foaming river,
Down the rapids of Pauwating,
Kwasind sailed with his companions,
In the stream he saw a beaver,
Saw Ahmeek, the King of Beavers,
Struggling with the rushing currents,
Rising, sinking in the water.

Without speaking, without pausing,
Kwasind leaped into the river,
Plunged beneath the bubbling surface,
Through the whirlpools chased the beaver,
Followed him among the islands,
Stayed so long beneath the water,
That his terrified companions
Cried, "Alas! good-by to Kwasind!
We shall never more see Kwasind!"
But he reappeared triumphant,
And upon his shining shoulders
Brought the beaver, dead and dripping,
Brought the King of all the Beavers.

And these two, as I have told you,
Were the friends of Hiawatha,

Chibiabos, the musician,
And the very strong man, Kwasind.
Long they lived in peace together,
Spake with naked hearts together,
Pondering much and much contriving
How the tribes of men might prosper.

VII

Hiawatha's Sailing

" GIVE me of your bark, O Birch-tree!
Of your yellow bark, O Birch-tree!
Growing by the rushing river,
Tall and stately in the valley!
I a light canoe will build me,
Build a swift Cheemaun for sailing,
That shall float upon the river,
Like a yellow leaf in Autumn,
Like a yellow water-lily!

  " Lay aside your cloak, O Birch-tree!
Lay aside your white-skin wrapper,
For the Summer-time is coming,
And the sun is warm in heaven,
And you need no white-skin wrapper!"

Thus aloud cried Hiawatha
In the solitary forest,
By the rushing Taquamenaw,
When the birds were singing gayly,
In the Moon of Leaves were singing,
And the sun, from sleep awaking,
Started up and said, " Behold me !
Geezis, the great Sun, behold me ! "
And the tree with all its branches
Rustled in the breeze of morning,
Saying, with a sigh of patience,
" Take my cloak, O Hiawatha ! "
With his knife the tree he girdled ;
Just beneath its lowest branches,
Just above the roots, he cut it,
Till the sap came oozing outward ;
Down the trunk, from top to bottom,
Sheer he cleft the bark asunder,
With a wooden wedge he raised it,
Stripped it from the trunk unbroken.
" Give me of your boughs, O Cedar !
Of your strong and pliant branches,
My canoe to make more steady,
Make more strong and firm beneath me ! "
Through the summit of the Cedar
Went a sound, a cry of horror,
Went a murmur of resistance ;

But it whispered, bending downward,
" Take my boughs, O Hiawatha ! "
    Down he hewed the boughs of cedar,
Shaped them straightway to a frame-work,
Like two bows he formed and shaped them,
Like two bended bows together.

    " Give me of your roots, O Tamarack !
Of your fibrous roots, O Larch-tree !
My canoe to bind together,
So to bind the ends together
That the water may not enter,
That the river may not wet me ! "
    And the Larch, with all its fibres,
Shivered in the air of morning,
Touched his forehead with its tassels,
Said, with one long sigh of sorrow,
" Take them all, O Hiawatha ! "

    From the earth he tore the fibres,
Tore the tough roots of the Larch-tree,
Closely sewed the bark together,
Bound it closely to the frame-work.
    " Give me of your balm, O Fir-tree !
Of your balsam and your resin,
So to close the seams together,
That the water may not enter,
That the river may not wet me ! "
    And the Fir-tree, tall and sombre,

Sobbed through all its robes of darkness,
Rattled like a shore with pebbles,
Answered wailing, answered weeping,
" Take my balm, O Hiawatha ! "
 And he took the tears of balsam,
Took the resin of the Fir-tree,
Smeared therewith each seam and fissure,
Made each crevice safe from water.

 " Give me of your quills, O Hedgehog !
All your quills, O Kagh, the Hedgehog !
I will make a necklace of them,
Make a girdle for my beauty,
And two stars to deck her bosom ! "
 From a hollow tree the Hedgehog
With his sleepy eyes looked at him,
Shot his shining quills, like arrows,
Saying with a drowsy murmur,
Through the tangle of his whiskers,
" Take my quills, O Hiawatha ! "
 From the ground the quills he gathered,
All the little shining arrows,
Stained them red and blue and yellow,
With the juice of roots and berries ;
Into his canoe he wrought them,
Round its waist a shining girdle,
Round its bows a gleaming necklace,
On its breast two stars resplendent.

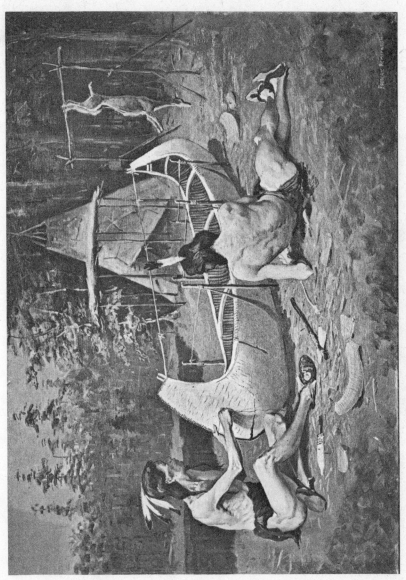

Thus the Birch Canoe was builded . . . .

In the bosom of the forest

Thus the Birch Canoe was builded
In the valley, by the river,
In the bosom of the forest;
And the forest's life was in it,
All its mystery and its magic,
All the lightness of the birch-tree,
All the toughness of the cedar,
All the larch's supple sinews;
And it floated on the river
Like a yellow leaf in Autumn,
Like a yellow water-lily.

Paddles none had Hiawatha,
Paddles none he had or needed,
For his thoughts as paddles served him,
And his wishes served to guide him;
Swift or slow at will he glided,
Veered to right or left at pleasure.

Then he called aloud to Kwasind,
To his friend, the strong man, Kwasind,
Saying, " Help me clear this river
Of its sunken logs and sand-bars."

Straight into the river Kwasind
Plunged as if he were an otter,
Dived as if he were a beaver,
Stood up to his waist in water,
To his arm-pits in the river,
Swam and shouted in the river,

Tugged at sunken logs and branches,
With his hands he scooped the sand-bars,
With his feet the ooze and tangle.
  And thus sailed my Hiawatha
Down the rushing Taquamenaw,
Sailed through all its bends and windings,
Sailed through all its deeps and shallows,
While his friend, the strong man, Kwasind,
Swam the deeps, the shallows waded.
  Up and down the river went they,
In and out among its islands,
Cleared its bed of root and sand-bar,
Dragged the dead trees from its channel,
Made its passage safe and certain,
Made a pathway for the people,
From its springs among the mountains,
To the waters of Pauwating,
To the bay of Taquamenaw.

VIII

Hiawatha's Fishing

Forth upon the Gitche Gumee,
On the shining Big-Sea-Water,
With his fishing-line of cedar,
Of the twisted bark of cedar,
Forth to catch the sturgeon Nahma,
Mishe-Nahma, King of Fishes,
In his birch canoe exulting
All alone went Hiawatha.

Through the clear, transparent water
He could see the fishes swimming
Far down in the depths below him;
See the yellow perch, the Sahwa,
Like a sunbeam in the water,
See the Shawgashee, the craw-fish,
Like a spider on the bottom,
On the white and sandy bottom.

At the stern sat Hiawatha,
With his fishing-line of cedar;
In his plumes the breeze of morning
Played as in the hemlock branches;
On the bows, with tail erected,
Sat the squirrel, Adjidaumo;
In his fur the breeze of morning
Played as in the prairie grasses.

On the white sand of the bottom
Lay the monster Mishe-Nahma,
Lay the sturgeon, King of Fishes;
Through his gills he breathed the water,
With his fins he fanned and winnowed,
With his tail he swept the sand-floor.

There he lay in all his armor;
On each side a shield to guard him,
Plates of bone upon his forehead,
Down his sides and back and shoulders
Plates of bone with spines projecting!

Painted was he with his war-paints,
Stripes of yellow, red, and azure,
Spots of brown and spots of sable ;
And he lay there on the bottom,
Fanning with his fins of purple,
As above him Hiawatha
In his birch canoe came sailing,
With his fishing-line of cedar.

" Take my bait," cried Hiawatha,
Down into the depths beneath him,
" Take my bait, O Sturgeon, Nahma !
Come up from below the water,
Let us see which is the stronger ! "
And he dropped his line of cedar
Through the clear, transparent water,
Waited vainly for an answer,
Long sat waiting for an answer,
And repeating loud and louder,
" Take my bait, O King of Fishes ! "

Quiet lay the sturgeon, Nahma,
Fanning slowly in the water,
Looking up at Hiawatha,
Listening to his call and clamor,
His unnecessary tumult,
Till he wearied of the shouting ;
And he said to the Kenozha,
To the pike, the Maskenozha,

"Take the bait of this rude fellow,
Break the line of Hiawatha!"
    In his fingers Hiawatha
Felt the loose line jerk and tighten;
As he drew it in, it tugged so
That the birch canoe stood endwise,
Like a birch log in the water,
With the squirrel, Adjidaumo,
Perched and frisking on the summit.

    Full of scorn was Hiawatha
When he saw the fish rise upward,
Saw the pike, the Maskenozha,
Coming nearer, nearer to him,
And he shouted through the water,
"Esa! esa! shame upon you!
You are but the pike, Kenozha,
You are not the fish I wanted,
You are not the King of Fishes!"
    Reeling downward to the bottom
Sank the pike in great confusion,
And the mighty sturgeon, Nahma,
Said to Ugudwash, the sun-fish,
To the bream, with scales of crimson,
"Take the bait of this great boaster,
Break the line of Hiawatha!"
    Slowly upward, wavering, gleaming,
Rose the Ugudwash, the sun-fish,

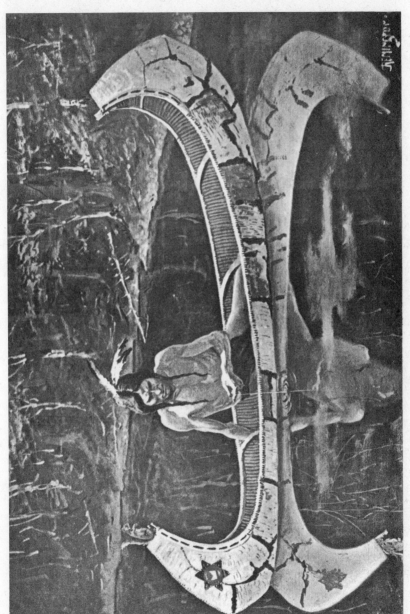

Long sat waiting for an answer

Seized the line of Hiawatha,
Swung with all his weight upon it,
Made a whirlpool in the water,
Whirled the birch canoe in circles,
Round and round in gurgling eddies,
Till the circles in the water
Reached the far-off sandy beaches,
Till the water-flags and rushes
Nodded on the distant margins.

But when Hiawatha saw him
Slowly rising through the water,
Lifting up his disk refulgent,
Loud he shouted in derision,
"Esa! esa! shame upon you!
You are Ugudwash, the sun-fish,
You are not the fish I wanted,
You are not the King of Fishes!"

Slowly downward, wavering, gleaming,
Sank the Ugudwash, the sun-fish,
And again the sturgeon, Nahma,
Heard the shout of Hiawatha,
Heard his challenge of defiance,
The unnecessary tumult,
Ringing far across the water.

From the white sand of the bottom
Up he rose with angry gesture,
Quivering in each nerve and fibre,

Clashing all his plates of armor,
Gleaming bright with all his war-paint;
In his wrath he darted upward,
Flashing leaped into the sunshine,
Opened his great jaws, and swallowed
Both canoe and Hiawatha.

Down into that darksome cavern
Plunged the headlong Hiawatha,
As a log on some black river
Shoots and plunges down the rapids,
Found himself in utter darkness,
Groped about in helpless wonder,
Till he felt a great heart beating,
Throbbing in that utter darkness.

And he smote it in his anger,
With his fist, the heart of Nahma,
Felt the mighty King of Fishes
Shudder through each nerve and fibre,
Heard the water gurgle round him
As he leaped and staggered through it,
Sick at heart, and faint and weary.

Crosswise then did Hiawatha
Drag his birch-canoe for safety,
Lest from out the jaws of Nahma,
In the turmoil and confusion,
Forth he might be hurled and perish.
And the squirrel, Adjidaumo,

Frisked and chattered very gayly,
Toiled and tugged with Hiawatha
Till the labor was completed.
Then said Hiawatha to him,
" O my little friend, the squirrel,
Bravely have you toiled to help me ;
Take the thanks of Hiawatha,
And the name which now he gives you ;
For hereafter and forever
Boys shall call you Adjidaumo,
Tail-in-air the boys shall call you ! "
And again the sturgeon, Nahma,
Gasped and quivered in the water,
Then was still, and drifted landward
Till he grated on the pebbles,
Till the listening Hiawatha
Heard him grate upon the margin,
Felt him strand upon the pebbles,
Knew that Nahma, King of Fishes,
Lay there dead upon the margin.

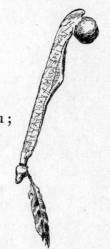

Then he heard a clang and flapping,
As of many wings assembling,
Heard a screaming and confusion,
As of birds of prey contending,
Saw a gleam of light above him,
Shining through the ribs of Nahma,
Saw the glittering eyes of sea-gulls,

Of Kayoshk, the sea-gulls, peering,
Gazing at him through the opening,
Heard them saying to each other,
" 'T is our brother, Hiawatha!"
    And he shouted from below them,
Cried exulting from the caverns:
" O ye sea-gulls! O my brothers!
I have slain the sturgeon, Nahma;
Make the rifts a little larger,
With your claws the openings widen,
Set me free from this dark prison,
And henceforward and forever
Men shall speak of your achievements,
Calling you Kayoshk, the sea-gulls,
Yes, Kayoshk, the Noble Scratchers!"
    And the wild and clamorous sea-gulls
Toiled with beak and claws together,
Made the rifts and openings wider
In the mighty ribs of Nahma,
And from peril and from prison,
From the body of the sturgeon,
From the peril of the water,
They released my Hiawatha.
    He was standing near his wigwam,
On the margin of the water,
And he called to old Nokomis,
Called and beckoned to Nokomis,

Pointed to the sturgeon, Nahma,
Lying lifeless on the pebbles,
With the sea-gulls feeding on him.
  "I have slain the Mishe-Nahma,
Slain the King of Fishes!" said he;
"Look! the sea-gulls feed upon him,
Yes, my friends Kayoshk, the sea-gulls;
Drive them not away, Nokomis,
They have saved me from great peril
In the body of the sturgeon,
Wait until their meal is ended,
Till their craws are full with feasting,
Till they homeward fly, at sunset,
To their nests among the marshes;
Then bring all your pots and kettles,
And make oil for us in Winter."

  And she waited till the sun set,
Till the pallid moon, the Night-sun,
Rose above the tranquil water,
Till Kayoshk, the sated sea-gulls,
From their banquet rose with clamor,
And across the fiery sunset
Winged their way to far-off islands,
To their nests among the rushes.
  To his sleep went Hiawatha,
And Nokomis to her labor,
Toiling patient in the moonlight,

Till the sun and moon changed places,
Till the sky was red with sunrise,
And Kayoshk, the hungry sea-gulls,
Came back from the reedy islands,
Clamorous for their morning banquet.

Three whole days and nights alternate
Old Nokomis and the sea-gulls
Stripped the oily flesh of Nahma,
Till the waves washed through the rib-bones,
Till the sea-gulls came no longer,
And upon the sands lay nothing
But the skeleton of Nahma.

IX

Hiawatha and the Pearl-Feather

On the shores of Gitche Gumee,
Of the shining Big-Sea-Water,
Stood Nokomis, the old woman,
Pointing with her finger westward,
O'er the water pointing westward,
To the purple clouds of sunset.

    Fiercely the red sun descending
Burned his way along the heavens,
Set the sky on fire behind him,
As war-parties, when retreating,

Burn the prairies on their war-trail;
And the moon, the Night-sun, eastward,
Suddenly starting from his ambush,
Followed fast those bloody footprints,
Followed in that fiery war-trail,
With its glare upon his features.

And Nokomis, the old woman,
Pointing with her finger westward,
Spake these words to Hiawatha:
"Yonder dwells the great Pearl-Feather,
Megissogwon, the Magician,
Manito of Wealth and Wampum,
Guarded by his fiery serpents,
Guarded by the black pitch-water.
You can see his fiery serpents,
The Kenabeek, the great serpents,
Coiling, playing in the water;
You can see the black pitch-water
Stretching far away beyond them,
To the purple clouds of sunset!

"He it was who slew my father,
By his wicked wiles and cunning,
When he from the moon descended,
When he came on earth to seek me.
He, the mightiest of Magicians,
Sends the fever from the marshes,
Sends the pestilential vapors,

Sends the poisonous exhalations,
Sends the white fog from the fen-lands,
Sends disease and death among us!
  "Take your bow, O Hiawatha,
Take your arrows, jasper-headed,
Take your war-club, Puggawaugun,
And your mittens, Minjekahwun,
And your birch-canoe for sailing,
And the oil of Mishe-Nahma,
So to smear its sides, that swiftly
You may pass the black pitch-water;
Slay this merciless magician,
Save the people from the fever
That he breathes across the fen-lands,
And avenge my father's murder!"
  Straightway then my Hiawatha
Armed himself with all his war-gear,
Launched his birch-canoe for sailing;
With his palm its sides he patted,
Said with glee, "Cheemaun, my darling,
O my Birch-canoe! leap forward,
Where you see the fiery serpents,
Where you see the black pitch-water!"
  Forward leaped Cheemaun exulting,
And the noble Hiawatha
Sang his war-song wild and woful,
And above him the war-eagle,

The Keneu, the great war-eagle,
Master of all fowls with feathers,
Screamed and hurtled through the heavens.
    Soon he reached the fiery serpents,
The Kenabeek, the great serpents,
Lying huge upon the water,
Sparkling, rippling in the water,
Lying coiled across the passage,
With their blazing crests uplifted,
Breathing fiery fogs and vapors,
So that none could pass beyond them.
    But the fearless Hiawatha
Cried aloud, and spake in this wise:
" Let me pass my way, Kenabeek,
    Let me go upon my journey ! "
And they answered, hissing fiercely,
With their fiery breath made answer :
" Back, go back !   O Shaugodaya !
    Back to old Nokomis, Faint-heart ! "
    Then the angry Hiawatha
Raised his mighty bow of ash-tree,
Seized his arrows, jasper-headed,
Shot them fast among the serpents ;
Every twanging of the bow-string
Was a war-cry and a death-cry,
Every whizzing of an arrow
Was a death-song of Kenabeek.

Weltering in the bloody water,
Dead lay all the fiery serpents,
And among them Hiawatha
Harmless sailed, and cried exulting :
" Onward, O Cheemaun, my darling !
Onward to the black pitch-water ! "
Then he took the oil of Nahma,
And the bows and sides anointed,
Smeared them well with oil, that swiftly
He might pass the black pitch-water.

All night long he sailed upon it,
Sailed upon that sluggish water,
Covered with its mould of ages,
Black with rotting water-rushes,
Rank with flags and leaves of lilies,
Stagnant, lifeless, dreary, dismal,
Lighted by the shimmering moonlight,
And by will-o'-the-wisps illumined,
Fires by ghosts of dead men kindled,
In their weary night-encampments.

All the air was white with moonlight,
All the water black with shadow,
And around him the Suggema,
The mosquito, sang his war-song,
And the fire-flies, Wah-wah-taysee,
Waved their torches to mislead him ;
And the bull-frog, the Dahinda,

Thrust his head into the moonlight,
Fixed his yellow eyes upon him,
Sobbed and sank beneath the surface ;
And anon a thousand whistles,
Answered over all the fen-lands,
And the heron, the Shuh-shuh-gah,
Far off on the reedy margin,
Heralded the hero's coming.

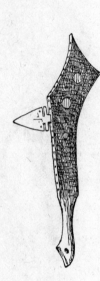

Westward thus fared Hiawatha,
Toward the realm of Megissogwon,
Toward the land of the Pearl-Feather,
Till the level moon stared at him,
In his face stared pale and haggard,
Till the sun was hot behind him,
Till it burned upon his shoulders,
And before him on the upland
He could see the Shining Wigwam
Of the Manito of Wampum,
Of the mightiest of Magicians.

Then once more Cheemaun he patted,
To his birch-canoe said, " Onward ! "
And it stirred in all its fibres,
And with one great bound of triumph
Leaped across the water-lilies,
Leaped through tangled flags and rushes,
And upon the beach beyond them
Dry-shod landed Hiawatha.

Straight he took his bow of ash-tree,
On the sand one end he rested,
With his knee he pressed the middle,
Stretched the faithful bow-string tighter,
Took an arrow, jasper-headed,
Shot it at the Shining Wigwam,
Sent it singing as a herald,
As a bearer of his message,
Of his challenge loud and lofty:
" Come forth from your lodge, Pearl-Feather!
Hiawatha waits your coming!"
Straightway from the Shining Wigwam

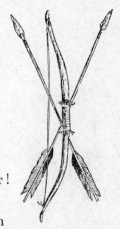

Came the mighty Megissogwon,
Tall of stature, broad of shoulder,
Dark and terrible in aspect,
Clad from head to foot in wampum,
Armed with all his warlike weapons,
Painted like the sky of morning,
Streaked with crimson, blue, and yellow,
Crested with great eagle-feathers,
Streaming upward, streaming outward.

" Well I know you, Hiawatha!"
Cried he in a voice of thunder,
In a tone of loud derision.
" Hasten back, O Shaugodaya!
Hasten back among the women,
Back to old Nokomis, Faint-heart!

I will slay you as you stand there,
As of old I slew her father! "
　But my Hiawatha answered,
Nothing daunted, fearing nothing :
" Big words do not smite like war-clubs,
Boastful breath is not a bow-string,
Taunts are not so sharp as arrows,
Deeds are better things than words are,
Actions mightier than boastings! "
　Then began the greatest battle
That the sun had ever looked on,
That the war-birds ever witnessed.
All a Summer's day it lasted,
From the sunrise to the sunset ;
For the shafts of Hiawatha
Harmless hit the shirt of wampum,
Harmless fell the blows he dealt it
With his mittens, Minjekahwun,
Harmless fell the heavy war-club ;
It could dash the rocks asunder,
But it could not break the meshes
Of that magic shirt of wampum.
　Till at sunset Hiawatha,
Leaning on his bow of ash-tree,
Wounded, weary, and desponding,
With his mighty war-club broken,
With his mittens torn and tattered,

Then began the greatest battle
That the sun had ever looked on

And three useless arrows only,
Paused to rest beneath a pine-tree,
From whose branches trailed the mosses,
And whose trunk was coated over
With the Dead-man's Moccasin-leather,
With the fungus white and yellow.

 Suddenly from the boughs above him
Sang the Mama, the woodpecker :
" Aim your arrows, Hiawatha,
At the head of Megissogwon,
Strike the tuft of hair upon it,
At their roots the long black tresses ;
There alone can he be wounded ! "

 Winged with feathers, tipped with jasper,
Swift flew Hiawatha's arrow,
Just as Megissogwon, stooping,
Raised a heavy stone to throw it.
Full upon the crown it struck him,
At the roots of his long tresses,
And he reeled and staggered forward,
Plunging like a wounded bison,
Yes, like Pezhekee, the bison,
When the snow is on the prairie.

 Swifter flew the second arrow,
In the pathway of the other,
Piercing deeper than the other,
Wounding sorer than the other ;

And the knees of Megissogwon
Shook like windy reeds beneath him,
Bent and trembled like the rushes.

But the third and latest arrow
Swiftest flew, and wounded sorest,
And the mighty Megissogwon
Saw the fiery eyes of Pauguk,
Saw the eyes of Death glare at him,
Heard his voice call in the darkness ;
At the feet of Hiawatha
Lifeless lay the great Pearl-Feather,
Lay the mightiest of Magicians.

Then the grateful Hiawatha
Called the Mama, the woodpecker,
From his perch among the branches
Of the melancholy pine-tree,
And, in honor of his service,
Stained with blood the tuft of feathers
On the little head of Mama ;
Even to this day he wears it,
Wears the tuft of crimson feathers,
As a symbol of his service.

Then he stripped the shirt of wampum
From the back of Megissogwon,
As a trophy of the battle,
As a signal of his conquest.
On the shore he left the body,

Half on land and half in water,
In the sand his feet were buried,
And his face was in the water.
And above him, wheeled and clamored
The Keneu, the great war-eagle,
Sailing round in narrower circles,
Hovering nearer, nearer, nearer.

From the wigwam Hiawatha
Bore the wealth of Megissogwon,
All his wealth of skins and wampum,
Furs of bison and of beaver,
Furs of sable and of ermine,
Wampum belts and strings and pouches,
Quivers wrought with beads of wampum,
Filled with arrows, silver-headed.

Homeward then he sailed exulting,
Homeward through the black pitch-water,
Homeward through the weltering serpents,
With the trophies of the battle,
With a shout and song of triumph.

On the shore stood old Nokomis,
On the shore stood Chibiabos,
And the very strong man, Kwasind,
Waiting for the hero's coming,
Listening to his songs of triumph.
And the people of the village
Welcomed him with songs and dances,

Made a joyous feast, and shouted:
" Honor be to Hiawatha !
He has slain the great Pearl-Feather,
Slain the mightiest of magicians,
Him, who sent the fiery fever,
Sent the white fog from the fen-lands,
Sent disease and death among us ! "

　　Ever dear to Hiawatha
Was the memory of Mama !
And in token of his friendship,
As a mark of his remembrance,
He adorned and decked his pipe-stem
With the crimson tuft of feathers,
With the blood-red crest of Mama.
But the wealth of Megissogwon,
All the trophies of the battle,
He divided with his people,
Shared it equally among them.

X

Hiawatha's Wooing

" As unto the bow the cord is,
  So unto the man is woman,
  Though she bends him, she obeys him,
  Though she draws him, yet she follows,
  Useless each without the other ! "
      Thus the youthful Hiawatha
  Said within himself and pondered,

Much perplexed by various feelings,
Listless, longing, hoping, fearing,
Dreaming still of Minnehaha,
Of the lovely Laughing Water,
In the land of the Dacotahs.
    " Wed a maiden of your people,"
Warning said the old Nokomis ;
" Go not eastward, go not westward,
For a stranger, whom we know not !
Like a fire upon the hearth-stone
Is a neighbor's homely daughter,
Like the starlight or the moonlight
Is the handsomest of strangers ! "
    Thus dissuading spake Nokomis,
And my Hiawatha answered
Only this : " Dear old Nokomis,
Very pleasant is the firelight,
But I like the starlight better,
Better do I like the moonlight ! "
    Gravely then said old Nokomis :
" Bring not here an idle maiden,
Bring not here a useless woman,
Hands unskilful, feet unwilling ;
Bring a wife with nimble fingers,
Heart and hand that move together,
Feet that run on willing errands ! "
    Smiling answered Hiawatha :

" In the land of the Dacotahs
Lives the Arrow-maker's daughter,
Minnehaha, Laughing Water,
Handsomest of all the women.
I will bring her to your wigwam,
She shall run upon your errands,
Be your starlight, moonlight, firelight,
Be the sunlight of my people ! "
   Still dissuading said Nokomis :
" Bring not to my lodge a stranger
From the land of the Dacotahs !
Very fierce are the Dacotahs,
Often is there war between us,
There are feuds yet unforgotten,
Wounds that ache and still may open ! "
   Laughing answered Hiawatha :
" For that reason, if no other,
Would I wed the fair Dacotah,
That our tribes might be united,
That old feuds might be forgotten,
And old wounds be healed forever ! "
   Thus departed Hiawatha
To the land of the Dacotahs,
To the land of handsome women ;
Striding over moor and meadow,
Through interminable forests,
Through uninterrupted silence.

With his moccasins of magic,
At each stride a mile he measured;
Yet the way seemed long before him,
And his heart outran his footsteps;
And he journeyed without resting,

Till he heard the cataract's laughter,
Heard the Falls of Minnehaha
Calling to him through the silence.
"Pleasant is the sound!" he murmured,
"Pleasant is the voice that calls me!"
On the outskirts of the forests,
'Twixt the shadow and the sunshine,
Herds of fallow deer were feeding,
But they saw not Hiawatha;
To his bow he whispered, "Fail not!"

To his arrow whispered, "Swerve not!"
Sent it singing on its errand,
To the red heart of the roebuck;
Threw the deer across his shoulder,
And sped forward without pausing.
At the doorway of his wigwam
Sat his ancient Arrow-maker,
In the land of the Dacotahs,
Making arrow-heads of jasper,
Arrow-heads of chalcedony.
At his side, in all her beauty,
Sat the lovely Minnehaha,

Sat his daughter, Laughing Water,
Plaiting mats of flags and rushes ;
Of the past the old man's thoughts were,
And the maiden's of the future.

He was thinking, as he sat there,
Of the days when with such arrows
He had struck the deer and bison,
On the Muskoday, the meadow ;
Shot the wild goose, flying southward,
On the wing, the clamorous Wawa ;
Thinking of the great war-parties,
How they came to buy his arrows,
Could not fight without his arrows.
Ah, no more such noble warriors
Could be found on earth as they were !
Now the men were all like women,
Only used their tongues for weapons !

She was thinking of a hunter,
From another tribe and country,
Young and tall and very handsome,
Who one morning, in the Spring-time,
Came to buy her father's arrows,
Sat and rested in the wigwam,
Lingered long about the doorway,
Looking back as he departed.
She had heard her father praise him,
Praise his courage and his wisdom ;

Would he come again for arrows
To the Falls of Minnehaha?
On the mat her hands lay idle,
And her eyes were very dreamy.

  Through their thoughts they heard a
    footstep,
Heard a rustling in the branches,
And with glowing cheek and forehead,
With the deer upon his shoulders,
Suddenly from out the woodlands
Hiawatha stood before them.

  Straight the ancient Arrow-maker
Looked up gravely from his labor,
Laid aside the unfinished arrow,
Bade him enter at the doorway,
Saying, as he rose to meet him,
"Hiawatha, you are welcome!"

  At the feet of Laughing Water
Hiawatha laid his burden,
Threw the red deer from his shoulders;
And the maiden looked up at him,
Looked up from her mat of rushes,
Said with gentle look and accent,
"You are welcome, Hiawatha!"

  Very spacious was the wigwam,
Made of deer-skins dressed and whitened,
With the Gods of the Dacotahs

Drawn and painted on its curtains,
And so tall the doorway, hardly
Hiawatha stooped to enter,
Hardly touched his eagle-feathers
As he entered at the doorway.

Then uprose the Laughing Water,
From the ground fair Minnehaha,
Laid aside her mat unfinished,
Brought forth food and set before them,
Water brought them from the brooklet,
Gave them food in earthen vessels,
Gave them drink in bowls of bass-wood,
Listened while the guest was speaking,
Listened while her father answered,
But not once her lips she opened,
Not a single word she uttered.

Yes, as in a dream she listened
To the words of Hiawatha,
As he talked of old Nokomis,
Who had nursed him in his childhood,
As he told of his companions,
Chibiabos, the musician,
And the very strong man, Kwasind,
And of happiness and plenty
In the land of the Ojibways,
In the pleasant land and peaceful.

" After many years of warfare,

Many years of strife and bloodshed,
There is peace between the Ojibways
And the tribe of the Dacotahs."
Thus continued Hiawatha,
And then added, speaking slowly,
" That this peace may last forever,
And our hands be clasped more closely,
And our hearts be more united,
Give me as my wife this maiden,
Minnehaha, Laughing Water,
Loveliest of Dacotah women ! "
    And the ancient Arrow-maker
Paused a moment ere he answered,
Smoked a little while in silence,
Looked at Hiawatha proudly,
Fondly looked at Laughing Water,
And made answer very gravely :
" Yes, if Minnehaha wishes ;
Let your heart speak, Minnehaha ! "

    And the lovely Laughing Water
Seemed more lovely as she stood there,
Neither willing nor reluctant,
As she went to Hiawatha,
Softly took the seat beside him,
While she said, and blushed to say it,
" I will follow you, my husband ! "
    This was Hiawatha's wooing !

" I will follow you, my husband !"

Thus it was he won the daughter
Of the ancient Arrow-maker,
In the land of the Dacotahs !
 From the wigwam he departed,
Leading with him Laughing Water;
Hand in hand they went together,
Through the woodland and the meadow,
Left the old man standing lonely
At the doorway of his wigwam,
Heard the Falls of Minnehaha
Calling to them from the distance,
Crying to them from afar off,
" Fare thee well, O Minnehaha ! "
 And the ancient Arrow-maker
Turned again unto his labor,
Sat down by his sunny doorway,
Murmuring to himself, and saying:
" Thus it is our daughters leave us,
 Those we love, and those who love us !
 Just when they have learned to help us,
 When we are old and lean upon them,
 Comes a youth with flaunting feathers,
 With his flute of reeds, a stranger
 Wanders piping through the village,
 Beckons to the fairest maiden,
 And she follows where he leads her,
 Leaving all things for the stranger ! "

Pleasant was the journey homeward,
Through interminable forests,
Over meadow, over mountain,
Over river, hill, and hollow.
Short it seemed to Hiawatha,
Though they journeyed very slowly,
Though his pace he checked and slackened
To the steps of Laughing Water.
　　Over wide and rushing rivers
In his arms he bore the maiden;
Light he thought her as a feather,
As the plume upon his head-gear;
Cleared the tangled pathway for her,
Bent aside the swaying branches,
Made at night a lodge of branches,
And a bed with boughs of hemlock,
And a fire before the doorway
With the dry cones of the pine-tree.
　　All the travelling winds went with them,
O'er the meadows, through the forest;
All the stars of night looked at them,
Watched with sleepless eyes their slumber;
From his ambush in the oak-tree
Peeped the squirrel, Adjidaumo,
Watched with eager eyes the lovers;
And the rabbit, the Wabasso,
Scampered from the path before them,

Peering, peeping from his burrow,
Sat erect upon his haunches,
Watched with curious eyes the lovers.
　　Pleasant was the journey homeward!
All the birds sang loud and sweetly
Songs of happiness and heart's-ease;
Sang the bluebird, the Owaissa,
" Happy are you, Hiawatha,
Having such a wife to love you! "
Sang the robin, the Opechee,
" Happy are you, Laughing Water,
Having such a noble husband! "
　　From the sky the sun benignant
Looked upon them through the branches,
Saying to them, " O my children,
Love is sunshine, hate is shadow,
Life is checkered shade and sunshine,
Rule by love, O Hiawatha! "
　　From the sky the moon looked at them,
Filled the lodge with mystic splendors,
Whispered to them, " O my children,
Day is restless, night is quiet,
Man imperious, woman feeble;
Half is mine, although I follow;
Rule by patience, Laughing Water! "
　　Thus it was they journeyed homeward;
Thus it was that Hiawatha

To the lodge of old Nokomis
Brought the moonlight, starlight, firelight,
Brought the sunshine of his people,
Minnehaha, Laughing Water,
Handsomest of all the women
In the land of the Dacotahs,
In the land of handsome women.

XI

Hiawatha's Wedding-Feast

You shall hear how Pau-Puk-Keewis,
How the handsome Yenadizze
Danced at Hiawatha's wedding ;
How the gentle Chibiabos,
He the sweetest of musicians,
Sang his songs of love and longing ;
How Iagoo, the great boaster,
He the marvellous story-teller,
Told his tales of strange adventure,
That the feast might be more joyous,
That the time might pass more gayly,
And the guests be more contented.

Sumptuous was the feast Nokomis
Made at Hiawatha's wedding ;
All the bowls were made of bass-wood,
White and polished very smoothly,
All the spoons of horn of bison,
Black and polished very smoothly.

She had sent through all the village
Messengers with wands of willow,
As a sign of invitation,
As a token of the feasting ;
And the wedding guests assembled,
Clad in all their richest raiment,
Robes of fur and belts of wampum,
Splendid with their paint and plumage,
Beautiful with beads and tassels.

First they ate the sturgeon, Nahma,
And the pike, the Maskenozha,
Caught and cooked by old Nokomis ;
Then on pemican they feasted,
Pemican and buffalo marrow,
Haunch of deer and hump of bison,
Yellow cakes of the Mondamin,
And the wild rice of the river.

But the gracious Hiawatha,
And the lovely Laughing Water,
And the careful old Nokomis,
Tasted not the food before them,

Only waited on the others,
Only served their guests in silence.

And when all the guests had finished,
Old Nokomis, brisk and busy,
From an ample pouch of otter,
Filled the red-stone pipes for smoking
With tobacco from the South-land,
Mixed with bark of the red willow,
And with herbs and leaves of fragrance.

Then she said, " O Pau-Puk-Keewis,
Dance for us your merry dances,
Dance the Beggar's Dance to please us,
That the feast may be more joyous,
That the time may pass more gayly,
And our guests be more contented ! "

Then the handsome Pau-Puk-Keewis,
He the idle Yenadizze,
He the merry mischief-maker,
Whom the people called the Storm-Fool,
Rose among the guests assembled.

Skilled was he in sports and pastimes,
In the merry dance of snow-shoes,
In the play of quoits and ball-play ;
Skilled was he in games of hazard,
In all games of skill and hazard,
Pugasaing, the Bowl and Counters,
Kuntassoo, the Game of Plum-stones.

Though the warriors called him Faint-Heart,
Called him coward, Shaugodaya,
Idler, gambler, Yenadizze,
Little heeded he their jesting,
Little cared he for their insults,
For the women and the maidens
Loved the handsome Pau-Puk-Keewis.

He was dressed in shirt of doeskin,
White and soft, and fringed with ermine,
All inwrought with beads of wampum;
He was dressed in deer-skin leggings,
Fringed with hedgehog quills and ermine,
And in moccasins of buck-skin,
Thick with quills and beads embroidered.
On his head were plumes of swan's down,
On his heels were tails of foxes,
In one hand a fan of feathers,
And a pipe was in the other.

Barred with streaks of red and yellow,
Streaks of blue and bright vermilion,
Shone the face of Pau-Puk-Keewis.
From his forehead fell his tresses,
Smooth, and parted like a woman's,
Shining bright with oil, and plaited,
Hung with braids of scented grasses,
As among the guests assembled,
To the sound of flutes and singing,

To the sound of drums and voices,
Rose the handsome Pau-Puk-Keewis,
And began his mystic dances.

First he danced a solemn measure,
Very slow in step and gesture,
In and out among the pine-trees,
Through the shadows and the sunshine,
Treading softly like a panther.
Then more swiftly and still swifter,
Whirling, spinning round in circles,
Leaping o'er the guests assembled,
Eddying round and round the wigwam,
Till the leaves went whirling with him,
Till the dust and wind together
Swept in eddies round about him.

Then along the sandy margin
Of the lake, the Big-Sea-Water,
On he sped with frenzied gestures,
Stamped upon the sand, and tossed it
Wildly in the air around him;
Till the wind became a whirlwind,
Till the sand was blown and sifted
Like great snowdrifts o'er the landscape,
Heaping all the shores with Sand Dunes,
Sand Hills of the Nagow Wudjoo!

Thus the merry Pau-Puk-Keewis
Danced his Beggar's Dance to please them,

And, returning, sat down laughing
There among the guests assembled,
Sat and fanned himself serenely
With his fan of turkey-feathers.
    Then they said to Chibiabos,
To the friend of Hiawatha,
To the sweetest of all singers,
To the best of all musicians,
"Sing to us, O Chibiabos!
Songs of love and songs of longing,
That the feast may be more joyous,
That the time may pass more gayly,
And our guests be more contented!"
    And the gentle Chibiabos
Sang in accents sweet and tender,
Sang in tones of deep emotion,
Songs of love and songs of longing;
Looking still at Hiawatha,
Looking at fair Laughing Water,
Sang he softly, sang in this wise:
    "Onaway! Awake, beloved!
Thou the wild-flower of the forest!
Thou the wild-bird of the prairie!
Thou with eyes so soft and fawn-like!
    "If thou only lookest at me,
I am happy, I am happy,
As the lilies of the prairie,
When they feel the dew upon them!

Through the shadows and the sunshine,
Treading softly like a panther

" Sweet thy breath is as the fragrance
Of the wild-flowers in the morning,
As their fragrance is at evening,
In the Moon when leaves are falling.

" Does not all the blood within me
Leap to meet thee, leap to meet thee,
As the springs to meet the sunshine,
In the Moon when nights are brightest?

" Onaway! my heart sings to thee,
Sings with joy when thou art near me,
As the sighing, singing branches
In the pleasant Moon of Strawberries!

" When thou art not pleased, beloved,
Then my heart is sad and darkened,
As the shining river darkens
When the clouds drop shadows on it!

" When thou smilest, my beloved,
Then my troubled heart is brightened,
As in sunshine gleam the ripples
That the cold wind makes in rivers.

" Smiles the earth, and smile the waters,
Smile the cloudless skies above us,
But I lose the way of smiling
When thou art no longer near me!

" I myself, myself! behold me!
Blood of my beating heart, behold me!
Oh awake, awake, beloved!
Onaway! awake, beloved!"

Thus the gentle Chibiabos
Sang his song of love and longing;
And Iagoo, the great boaster,
He the marvellous story-teller,
He the friend of old Nokomis,
Jealous of the sweet musician,
Jealous of the applause they gave him,
Saw in all the eyes around him,
Saw in all their looks and gestures,
That the wedding guests assembled
Longed to hear his pleasant stories,
His immeasurable falsehoods.

Very boastful was Iagoo;
Never heard he an adventure
But himself had met a greater;
Never any deed of daring
But himself had done a bolder;
Never any marvellous story
But himself could tell a stranger.

Would you listen to his boasting,
Would you only give him credence,
No one ever shot an arrow
Half so far and high as he had;
Ever caught so many fishes,
Ever killed so many reindeer,
Ever trapped so many beaver!
None could run so fast as he could,

None could dive so deep as he could,
None could swim so far as he could;
None had made so many journeys,
None had seen so many wonders,
As this wonderful Iagoo,
As this marvellous story-teller!

Thus his name became a by-word
And a jest among the people;
And whene'er a boastful hunter
Praised his own address too highly,
Or a warrior, home returning,
Talked too much of his achievements,
All his hearers cried, "Iagoo!
Here 's Iagoo come among us!"

He it was who carved the cradle
Of the little Hiawatha,
Carved its framework out of linden,
Bound it strong with reindeer sinews;
He it was who taught him later
How to make his bows and arrows,
How to make the bows of ash-tree,
And the arrows of the oak-tree.
So among the guests assembled
At my Hiawatha's wedding
Sat Iagoo, old and ugly,
Sat the marvellous story-teller.

And they said, " O good Iagoo,

Tell us now a tale of wonder,
Tell us of some strange adventure,
That the feast may be more joyous,
That the time may pass more gayly,
And our guests be more contented!"
    And Iagoo answered straightway,
"You shall hear a tale of wonder,
You shall hear the strange adventures
Of Osseo, the Magician,
From the Evening Star descended."

XII

The Son of the Evening Star

Can it be the sun descending
O'er the level plain of water?
Or the Red Swan floating, flying,
Wounded by the magic arrow,
Staining all the waves with crimson,

With the crimson of its life-blood,
Filling all the air with splendor,
With the splendor of its plumage?
    Yes; it is the sun descending,
Sinking down into the water;
All the sky is stained with purple,
All the water flushed with crimson!
No; it is the Red Swan floating,
Diving down beneath the water;
To the sky its wings are lifted,
With its blood the waves are reddened!
    Over it the Star of Evening
Melts and trembles through the purple,
Hangs suspended in the twilight.
No; it is a bead of wampum
On the robes of the Great Spirit
As he passes through the twilight,
Walks in silence through the heavens.
    This with joy beheld Iagoo
And he said in haste: "Behold it!
See the sacred Star of Evening!
You shall hear a tale of wonder,
Hear the story of Osseo,
Son of the Evening Star, Osseo!
    "Once, in days no more remembered,
Ages nearer the beginning,
When the heavens were closer to us,

And the Gods were more familiar,
In the North-land lived a hunter,
With ten young and comely daughters,
Tall and lithe as wands of willow;
Only Oweenee, the youngest,
She the wilful and the wayward,
She the silent, dreamy maiden,
Was the fairest of the sisters.

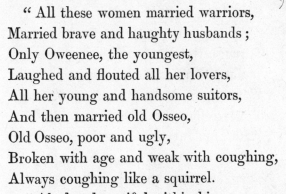

" All these women married warriors,
Married brave and haughty husbands;
Only Oweenee, the youngest,
Laughed and flouted all her lovers,
All her young and handsome suitors,
And then married old Osseo,
Old Osseo, poor and ugly,
Broken with age and weak with coughing,
Always coughing like a squirrel.

" Ah, but beautiful within him
Was the spirit of Osseo,
From the Evening Star descended,
Star of Evening, Star of Woman,
Star of tenderness and passion!
All its fire was in his bosom,
All its beauty in his spirit,
All its mystery in his being,
All its splendor in his language!

" And her lovers, the rejected,

Handsome men with belts of wampum,
Handsome men with paint and feathers,
Pointed at her in derision,
Followed her with jest and laughter.
But she said: 'I care not for you,
Care not for your belts of wampum,
Care not for your paint and feathers,
Care not for your jests and laughter;
I am happy with Osseo!'

"Once to some great feast invited,
Through the damp and dusk of evening,
Walked together the ten sisters,
Walked together with their husbands;
Slowly followed old Osseo,
With fair Oweenee beside him;
All the others chatted gayly,
These two only walked in silence.

"At the western sky Osseo
Gazed intent, as if imploring,
Often stopped and gazed imploring
At the trembling Star of Evening,
At the tender Star of Woman;
And they heard him murmur softly,
' *Ah, showain nemeshin, Nosa!*
Pity, pity me, my father!'

" 'Listen!' said the eldest sister,
' He is praying to his father!
What a pity that the old man

And her lovers, the rejected, ...
Handsome men with paint and feathers

Does not stumble in the pathway,
Does not break his neck by falling!'
And they laughed till all the forest
Rang with their unseemly laughter.

" On their pathway through the woodland
Lay an oak, by storms uprooted,
Lay the great trunk of an oak-tree,
Buried half in leaves and mosses,
Mouldering, crumbling, huge and hollow.
And Osseo, when he saw it,
Gave a shout, a cry of anguish,
Leaped into its yawning cavern,
At one end went in an old man,
Wasted, wrinkled, old, and ugly;
From the other came a young man,
Tall and straight and strong and handsome.

" Thus Osseo was transfigured,
Thus restored to youth and beauty;
But, alas for good Osseo,
And for Oweenee, the faithful!
Strangely, too, was she transfigured.
Changed into a weak old woman,
With a staff she tottered onward,
Wasted, wrinkled, old, and ugly!
And the sisters and their husbands
Laughed until the echoing forest
Rang with their unseemly laughter.

" But Osseo turned not from her,

Walked with slower step beside her,
Took her hand, as brown and withered
As an oak-leaf is in Winter,
Called her sweetheart, Nenemoosha,
Soothed her with soft words of kindness,
Till they reached the lodge of feasting,
Till they sat down in the wigwam,
Sacred to the Star of Evening,
To the tender Star of Woman.

" Wrapt in visions, lost in dreaming,
At the banquet sat Osseo ;
All were merry, all were happy,
All were joyous but Osseo.
Neither food nor drink he tasted,
Neither did he speak nor listen,
But as one bewildered sat he,
Looking dreamily and sadly,
First at Oweenee, then upward
At the gleaming sky above them.

"Then a voice was heard, a whisper,
Coming from the starry distance,
Coming from the empty vastness,
Low, and musical, and tender ;
And the voice said : ' O Osseo !
O my son, my best beloved !
Broken are the spells that bound you,
All the charms of the magician,

All the magic powers of evil;
Come to me; ascend, Osseo!
 " ' Taste the food that stands before you:
It is blessed and enchanted,
It has magic virtues in it,
It will change you to a spirit.
All your bowls and all your kettles
Shall be wood and clay no longer;
But the bowls be changed to wampum,
And the kettles shall be silver;
They shall shine like shells of scarlet,
Like the fire shall gleam and glimmer.

 " ' And the women shall no longer
Bear the dreary doom of labor,
But be changed to birds, and glisten
With the beauty of the starlight,
Painted with the dusky splendors
Of the skies and clouds of evening ! '
 " What Osseo heard as whispers,
What as words he comprehended,
Was but music to the others,
Music as of birds afar off,
Of the whippoorwill afar off,
Of the lonely Wawonaissa
Singing in the darksome forest.

 " Then the lodge began to tremble,
Straight began to shake and tremble,

And they felt it rising, rising,
Slowly through the air ascending,
From the darkness of the tree-tops
Forth into the dewy starlight,
Till it passed the topmost branches;
And behold! the wooden dishes
All were changed to shells of scarlet!
And behold! the earthen kettles
All were changed to bowls of silver!
And the roof-poles of the wigwam
Were as glittering rods of silver,
And the roof of bark upon them
As the shining shards of beetles.

" Then Osseo gazed around him,
And he saw the nine fair sisters,
All the sisters and their husbands,
Changed to birds of various plumage.
Some were jays and some were magpies,
Others thrushes, others blackbirds;
And they hopped, and sang, and twittered,
Perked and fluttered all their feathers.
Strutted in their shining plumage,
And their tails like fans unfolded.

" Only Oweenee, the youngest,
Was not changed, but sat in silence,
Wasted, wrinkled, old, and ugly,
Looking sadly at the others;

Till Osseo, gazing upward,
Gave another cry of anguish,
Such a cry as he had uttered
By the oak-tree in the forest.

  "Then returned her youth and beauty,
And her soiled and tattered garments
Were transformed to robes of ermine,
And her staff became a feather,
Yes, a shining silver feather!

  "And again the wigwam trembled,
Swayed and rushed through airy currents,
Through transparent cloud and vapor,
And amid celestial splendors
On the Evening Star alighted,
As a snow-flake falls on snow-flake,
As a leaf drops on a river,
As the thistle-down on water.

  "Forth with cheerful words of welcome
Came the father of Osseo,
He with radiant locks of silver,
He with eyes serene and tender.
And he said: 'My son, Osseo,
Hang the cage of birds you bring there,
Hang the cage with rods of silver,
And the birds with glistening feathers,
At the doorway of my wigwam.'

  "At the door he hung the bird-cage,

And they entered in and gladly
Listened to Osseo's father,
Ruler of the Star of Evening,
As he said: ' O my Osseo!
I have had compassion on you,
Given you back your youth and beauty,
Into birds of various plumage
Changed your sisters and their husbands;
Changed them thus because they mocked
    you
In the figure of the old man,
In that aspect sad and wrinkled,
Could not see your heart of passion,
Could not see your youth immortal;
Only Oweenee, the faithful,
Saw your naked heart and loved you.

  " ' In the lodge that glimmers yonder,
In the little star that twinkles
Through the vapors, on the left hand,
Lives the envious Evil Spirit,
The Wabeno, the magician,
Who transformed you to an old man.
Take heed lest his beams fall on you,
For the rays he darts around him
Are the power of his enchantment,
Are the arrows that he uses.'

  " Many years, in peace and quiet,

On the peaceful Star of Evening
Dwelt Osseo with his father;
Many years, in song and flutter,
At the doorway of the wigwam,
Hung the cage with rods of silver,
And fair Oweenee, the faithful,
Bore a son unto Osseo,
With the beauty of his mother,
With the courage of his father.

" And the boy grew up and prospered,
And Osseo, to delight him,
Made him little bows and arrows,
Opened the great cage of silver,
And let loose his aunts and uncles,
All those birds with glossy feathers,
For his little son to shoot at.

" Round and round they wheeled and
    darted,
Filled the Evening Star with music,
With their songs of joy and freedom;
Filled the Evening Star with splendor,
With the fluttering of their plumage;
Till the boy, the little hunter,
Bent his bow and shot an arrow,
Shot a swift and fatal arrow,
And a bird, with shining feathers,
At his feet fell wounded sorely.

"But, O wondrous transformation!
'T was no bird he saw before him,
'T was a beautiful young woman,
With the arrow in her bosom!
  "When her blood fell on the planet,
On the sacred Star of Evening,
Broken was the spell of magic,
Powerless was the strange enchantment,
And the youth, the fearless bowman,
Suddenly felt himself descending,
Held by unseen hands, but sinking
Downward through the empty spaces,
Downward through the clouds and vapors,
Till he rested on an island,
On an island, green and grassy,
Yonder in the Big-Sea-Water.
  "After him he saw descending
All the birds with shining feathers,
Fluttering, falling, wafted downward,
Like the painted leaves of Autumn;
And the lodge with poles of silver,
With its roof like wings of beetles,
Like the shining shards of beetles,
By the winds of heaven uplifted,
Slowly sank upon the island,
Bringing back the good Osseo,
Bringing Oweenee, the faithful.

" Then the birds, again transfigured,
Reassumed the shape of mortals,
Took their shape, but not their stature;
They remained as Little People,
Like the pygmies, the Puk-Wudjies,
And on pleasant nights of Summer,
When the Evening Star was shining,
Hand in hand they danced together
On the island's craggy headlands,
On the sand-beach low and level.

" Still their glittering lodge is seen there,
On the tranquil Summer evenings,
And upon the shore the fisher
Sometimes hears their happy voices,
Sees them dancing in the starlight ! "

When the story was completed,
When the wondrous tale was ended,
Looking round upon his listeners,
Solemnly Iagoo added :
" There are great men, I have known such,
Whom their people understand not,
Whom they even make a jest of,
Scoff and jeer at in derision.
From the story of Osseo
Let us learn the fate of jesters ! "

All the wedding guests delighted
Listened to the marvellous story,

Listened laughing and applauding,
And they whispered to each other:
" Does he mean himself, I wonder?
And are we the aunts and uncles?"
    Then again sang Chibiabos,
Sang a song of love and longing,
In those accents sweet and tender,
In those tones of pensive sadness,
Sang a maiden's lamentation
For her lover, her Algonquin.
    " When I think of my beloved,
Ah me! think of my beloved,
When my heart is thinking of him,
O my sweetheart, my Algonquin!

    " Ah me! when I parted from him,
Round my neck he hung the wampum,
As a pledge, the snow-white wampum,
O my sweetheart, my Algonquin!
    " I will go with you, he whispered,
Ah me! to your native country;
Let me go with you, he whispered,
O my sweetheart, my Algonquin!
    " Far away, away, I answered,
Very far away, I answered,
Ah me! is my native country,
O my sweetheart, my Algonquin!
    " When I looked back to behold him,

Where we parted, to behold him,
After me he still was gazing,
O my sweetheart, my Algonquin!
    " By the tree he still was standing,
By the fallen tree was standing,
That had dropped into the water,
O my sweetheart, my Algonquin!
    " When I think of my beloved,
Ah me! think of my beloved,
When my heart is thinking of him,
O my sweetheart, my Algonquin!"
    Such was Hiawatha's Wedding,
Such the dance of Pau-Puk-Keewis,
Such the story of Iagoo,
Such the songs of Chibiabos;
Thus the wedding banquet ended,
And the wedding guests departed,
Leaving Hiawatha happy
With the night and Minnehaha.

XIII

𝔅𝔩𝔢𝔰𝔰𝔦𝔫𝔤 𝔱𝔥𝔢 ℭ𝔬𝔯𝔫𝔣𝔦𝔢𝔩𝔡𝔰

Sing, O Song of Hiawatha,
Of the happy days that followed,
In the land of the Ojibways,
In the pleasant land and peaceful!
Sing the mysteries of Mondamin,
Sing the Blessing of the Cornfields!
　　Buried was the bloody hatchet,
Buried was the dreadful war-club,

Buried were all warlike weapons,
And the war-cry was forgotten.
There was peace among the nations;
Unmolested roved the hunters,
Built the birch canoe for sailing,
Caught the fish in lake and river,
Shot the deer and trapped the beaver;
Unmolested worked the women,
Made their sugar from the maple,
Gathered wild rice in the meadows,
Dressed the skins of deer and beaver.

    All around the happy village
Stood the maize-fields, green and shining,
Waved the green plumes of Mondamin,
Waved his soft and sunny tresses,
Filling all the land with plenty.
'T was the women who in Spring-time
Planted the broad fields and fruitful,
Buried in the earth Mondamin;
'T was the women who in Autumn
Stripped the yellow husks of harvest,
Stripped the garments from Mondamin,
Even as Hiawatha taught them.

    Once, when all the maize was planted,
Hiawatha, wise and thoughtful,
Spake and said to Minnehaha,
To his wife, the Laughing Water:

" You shall bless to-night the cornfields,
Draw a magic circle round them,
To protect them from destruction,
Blast of mildew, blight of insect,
Wagemin, the thief of cornfields,
Paimosaid, who steals the maize-ear !

" In the night, when all is silence,
In the night, when all is darkness,
When the Spirit of Sleep, Nepahwin,
Shuts the doors of all the wigwams,
So that not an ear can hear you,

So that not an eye can see you,
Rise up from your bed in silence,
Lay aside your garments wholly,
Walk around the fields you planted,
Round the borders of the cornfields,
Covered by your tresses only,
Robed with darkness as a garment.

" Thus the fields shall be more fruitful,
And the passing of your footsteps
Draw a magic circle round them,
So that neither blight nor mildew,
Neither burrowing worm nor insect,
Shall pass o'er the magic circle ;
Not the dragon-fly, Kwo-ne-she,
Nor the spider, Subbekashe,
Nor the grasshopper, Pah-puk-keena,

'Twas the women who in Autumn
Stripped the yellow husks of harvest

Nor the mighty caterpillar,
Way-muk-kwana, with the bear-skin,
King of all the caterpillars!"
 On the tree-tops near the cornfields
Sat the hungry crows and ravens,
Kahgahgee, the King of Ravens,
With his band of black marauders.
And they laughed at Hiawatha,
Till the tree-tops shook with laughter,
With their melancholy laughter,
At the words of Hiawatha.
"Hear him!" said they; "hear the Wise
  Man,
Hear the plots of Hiawatha!"
 When the noiseless night descended
Broad and dark o'er field and forest,
When the mournful Wawonaissa,
Sorrowing sang among the hemlocks,
And the Spirit of Sleep, Nepahwin,
Shut the doors of all the wigwams,
From her bed rose Laughing Water,
Laid aside her garments wholly,
And with darkness clothed and guarded,
Unashamed and unaffrighted,
Walked securely round the cornfields,
Drew the sacred, magic circle
Of her footprints round the cornfields.

No one but the Midnight only
Saw her beauty in the darkness,
No one but the Wawonaissa
Heard the panting of her bosom ;
Guskewau, the darkness, wrapped her
Closely in his sacred mantle,
So that none might see her beauty,
So that none might boast, " I saw her ! "
    On the morrow, as the day dawned,
Kahgahgee, the King of Ravens,
Gathered all his black marauders,
Crows and blackbirds, jays and ravens,
Clamorous on the dusky tree-tops,
And descended, fast and fearless,
On the fields of Hiawatha,
On the grave of the Mondamin.

    " We will drag Mondamin," said they,
" From the grave where he is buried,
Spite of all the magic circles
Laughing Water draws around it,
Spite of all the sacred footprints
Minnehaha stamps upon it ! "
    But the wary Hiawatha,
Ever thoughtful, careful, watchful,
Had o'erheard the scornful laughter,
When they mocked him from the tree-tops.
" Kaw ! " he said, " my friends the ravens !

Kahgahgee, my King of Ravens!
I will teach you all a lesson
That shall not be soon forgotten!"
   He had risen before the daybreak,
He had spread o'er all the cornfields
Snares to catch the black marauders,
And was lying now in ambush
In the neighboring grove of pine-trees,
Waiting for the crows and blackbirds,
Waiting for the jays and ravens.

   Soon they came with caw and clamor,
Rush of wings and cry of voices,
To their work of devastation,
Settling down upon the cornfields,
Delving deep with beak and talon,
For the body of Mondamin.
And with all their craft and cunning,
All their skill in wiles of warfare,
They perceived no danger near them,
Till their claws became entangled,
Till they found themselves imprisoned
In the snares of Hiawatha.

   From his place of ambush came he,
Striding terrible among them,
And so awful was his aspect
That the bravest quailed with terror.
Without mercy he destroyed them

Right and left, by tens and twenties,
And their wretched, lifeless bodies
Hung aloft on poles for scarecrows
Round the consecrated cornfields,
As a signal of his vengeance,
As a warning to marauders.

Only Kahgahgee, the leader,
Kahgahgee, the King of Ravens,
He alone was spared among them
As a hostage for his people.
With his prisoner-string he bound him,
Led him captive to his wigwam,
Tied him fast with cords of elm-bark
To the ridge-pole of his wigwam.

"Kahgahgee, my raven!" said he,
"You the leader of the robbers,
You the plotter of this mischief,
The contriver of this outrage,
I will keep you, I will hold you,
As a hostage for your people,
As a pledge of good behavior!"

And he left him, grim and sulky,
Sitting in the morning sunshine
On the summit of the wigwam,
Croaking fiercely his displeasure,
Flapping his great sable pinions,
Vainly struggling for his freedom,
Vainly calling on his people!

Summer passed, and Shawondasee
Breathed his sighs o'er all the landscape,
From the South-land sent his ardors,
Wafted kisses warm and tender;
And the maize-field grew and ripened,
Till it stood in all the splendor
Of its garments green and yellow,
Of its tassels and its plumage,
And the maize-ears full and shining
Gleamed from bursting sheaths of verdure.
    Then Nokomis, the old woman,
Spake, and said to Minnehaha:
" 'T is the Moon when leaves are falling;
All the wild rice has been gathered,
And the maize is ripe and ready;
Let us gather in the harvest,
Let us wrestle with Mondamin,
Strip him of his plumes and tassels,
Of his garments green and yellow!"
    And the merry Laughing Water
Went rejoicing from the wigwam,
With Nokomis, old and wrinkled,
And they called the women round them,
Called the young men and the maidens,
To the harvest of the cornfields,
To the husking of the maize-ear.
    On the border of the forest,
Underneath the fragrant pine-trees,

Sat the old men and the warriors
Smoking in the pleasant shadow.
In uninterrupted silence
Looked they at the gamesome labor
Of the young men and the women;
Listened to their noisy talking,
To their laughter and their singing,
Heard them chattering like the magpies,
Heard them laughing like the blue-jays,
Heard them singing like the robins.

And whene'er some lucky maiden
Found a red ear in the husking,
Found a maize-ear red as blood is,
" Nushka ! " cried they all together,
" Nushka ! you shall have a sweetheart,
You shall have a handsome husband ! "
" Ugh ! " the old men all responded
From their seats beneath the pine-trees.

And whene'er a youth or maiden
Found a crooked ear in husking,
Found a maize-ear in the husking
Blighted, mildewed, or misshapen,
Then they laughed and sang together,
Crept and limped about the cornfields,
Mimicked in their gait and gestures
Some old man, bent almost double,
Singing singly or together:

" Wagemin, the thief of cornfields!
    Paimosaid, who steals the maize-ear! "
        Till the cornfields rang with laughter,
    Till from Hiawatha's wigwam
    Kahgahgee, the King of Ravens,
    Screamed and quivered in his anger,
    And from all the neighboring tree-tops
    Cawed and croaked the black marauders.
" Ugh! " the old men all responded,
    From their seats beneath the pine-trees!

XIV

Picture-Writing

In those days said Hiawatha,
"Lo! how all things fade and perish!
From the memory of the old men
Pass away the great traditions,
The achievements of the warriors,
The adventures of the hunters,
All the wisdom of the Medas,
All the craft of the Wabenos,
All the marvellous dreams and visions
Of the Jossakeeds, the Prophets!

"Great men die and are forgotten,
Wise men speak; their words of wisdom

Perish in the ears that hear them,
Do not reach the generations
That, as yet unborn, are waiting
In the great, mysterious darkness
Of the speechless days that shall be !
  " On the grave-posts of our fathers
Are no signs, no figures painted ;
Who are in those graves we know not,
Only know they are our fathers.
Of what kith they are and kindred,
From what old, ancestral Totem,
Be it Eagle, Bear, or Beaver,
They descended, this we know not,
Only know they are our fathers.

  " Face to face we speak together,
But we cannot speak when absent,
Cannot send our voices from us
To the friends that dwell afar off ;
Cannot send a secret message,
But the bearer learns our secret,
May pervert it, may betray it,
May reveal it unto others."
  Thus said Hiawatha, walking
In the solitary forest,
Pondering, musing in the forest,
On the welfare of his people.
  From his pouch he took his colors,

Took his paints of different colors,
On the smooth bark of a birch-tree
Painted many shapes and figures,
Wonderful and mystic figures,
And each figure had a meaning,
Each some word or thought suggested.

Gitche Manito the Mighty,
He, the Master of Life, was painted
As an egg, with points projecting
To the four winds of the heavens.
Everywhere is the Great Spirit,
Was the meaning of this symbol.

Mitche Manito the Mighty,
He the dreadful Spirit of Evil,
As a serpent was depicted,
As Kenabeek, the great serpent.
Very crafty, very cunning,
Is the creeping Spirit of Evil,
Was the meaning of this symbol.

Life and Death he drew as circles,
Life was white, but Death was darkened;
Sun and moon and stars he painted,
Man and beast, and fish and reptile,
Forests, mountains, lakes, and rivers.

For the earth he drew a straight line,
For the sky a bow above it;
White the space between for daytime,

Filled with little stars for night-time;
On the left a point for sunrise,
On the right a point for sunset,
On the top a point for noontide,
And for rain and cloudy weather
Waving lines descending from it.

    Footprints pointing towards a wigwam
Were a sign of invitation,
Were a sign of guests assembling;
Bloody hands with palms uplifted
Were a symbol of destruction,
Were a hostile sign and symbol.

    All these things did Hiawatha
Show unto his wondering people,
And interpreted their meaning,
And he said : " Behold, your grave-posts
Have no mark, no sign, nor symbol.
Go and paint them all with figures;
Each one with its household symbol,
With its own ancestral Totem;
So that those who follow after
May distinguish them and know them."

    And they painted on the grave-posts
On the graves yet unforgotten,
Each his own ancestral Totem,
Each the symbol of his household;
Figures of the Bear and Reindeer,

Of the Turtle, Crane, and Beaver,
Each inverted as a token
That the owner was departed,
That the chief who bore the symbol
Lay beneath in dust and ashes.

And the Jossakeeds, the Prophets,
The Wabenos, the Magicians,
And the Medicine-men, the Medas,
Painted upon bark and deer-skin
Figures for the songs they chanted,
For each song a separate symbol,
Figures mystical and awful,
Figures strange and brightly colored;
And each figure had its meaning,
Each some magic song suggested.

The Great Spirit, the Creator,
Flashing light through all the heaven;
The Great Serpent, the Kenabeek,
With his bloody crest erected,
Creeping, looking into heaven;
In the sky the sun, that listens,
And the moon eclipsed and dying;
Owl and eagle, crane and hen-hawk,
And the cormorant, bird of magic;

Headless men, that walk the heavens,
Bodies lying pierced with arrows,
Bloody hands of death uplifted,

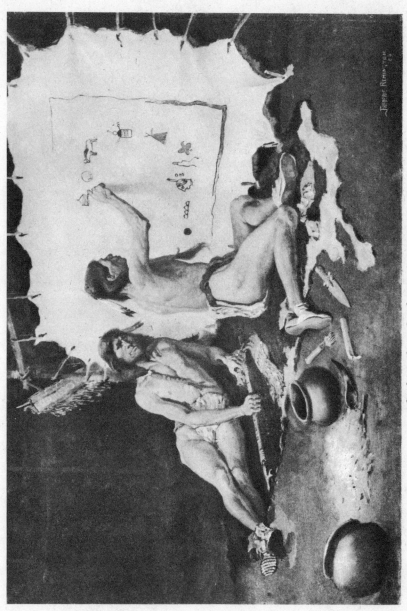

Such as these the shapes they painted
On the birch-bark and the deer-skin

Flags on graves, and great war-captains
Grasping both the earth and heaven!
  Such as these the shapes they painted
On the birch-bark and the deer-skin;
Songs of war and songs of hunting,
Songs of medicine and of magic,
All were written in these figures,
For each figure had its meaning,
Each its separate song recorded.

  Nor forgotten was the Love-Song,
The most subtle of all medicines,
The most potent spell of magic,
Dangerous more than war or hunting!
Thus the Love-Song was recorded,
Symbol and interpretation.

  First a human figure standing,
Painted in the brightest scarlet;
'T is the lover, the musician,
And the meaning is, " My painting
Makes me powerful over others."

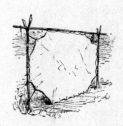

  Then the figure seated, singing,
Playing on a drum of magic,
And the interpretation, " Listen!
'T is my voice you hear, my singing!"
  Then the same red figure seated
In the shelter of a wigwam,
And the meaning of the symbol,

"I will come and sit beside you
In the mystery of my passion!"
    Then two figures, man and woman,
Standing hand in hand together
With their hands so clasped together
That they seemed in one united,
And the words thus represented
Are, "I see your heart within you,
And your cheeks are red with blushes!"
    Next the maiden on an island,
In the centre of an island;
And the song this shape suggested
Was, "Though you were at a distance,
Were upon some far-off island,
Such the spell I cast upon you,
Such the magic power of passion,
I could straightway draw you to me!"
    Then the figure of the maiden
Sleeping, and the lover near her,
Whispering to her in her slumbers,
Saying, "Though you were far from me
In the land of Sleep and Silence,
Still the voice of love would reach you!"
    And the last of all the figures
Was a heart within a circle,
Drawn within a magic circle;
And the image had this meaning:

"Naked lies your heart before me,
To your naked heart I whisper!"
Thus it was that Hiawatha,
In his wisdom, taught the people
All the mysteries of painting,
All the art of Picture-Writing,
On the smooth bark of the birch-tree,
On the white skin of the reindeer,
On the grave-posts of the village.

XV

Hiawatha's Lamentation

In those days the Evil Spirits,
All the Manitos of mischief,
Fearing Hiawatha's wisdom,
And his love for Chibiabos,
Jealous of their faithful friendship,
And their noble words and actions,
Made at length a league against them,
To molest them and destroy them.
  Hiawatha, wise and wary,
Often said to Chibiabos,

"O my brother! do not leave me,
Lest the Evil Spirits harm you!"
Chibiabos, young and heedless,
Laughing shook his coal-black tresses,
Answered ever sweet and childlike,
"Do not fear for me, O brother!
Harm and evil come not near me!"
  Once when Peboan, the Winter,
Roofed with ice the Big-Sea-Water,
When the snow-flakes, whirling downward,
Hissed among the withered oak-leaves,
Changed the pine-trees into wigwams,
Covered all the earth with silence, —
Armed with arrows, shod with snow-shoes,
Heeding not his brother's warning,
Fearing not the Evil Spirits,
Forth to hunt the deer with antlers
All alone went Chibiabos.
Right across the Big-Sea-Water
Sprang with speed the deer before him.
With the wind and snow he followed,
O'er the treacherous ice he followed,
Wild with all the fierce commotion
And the rapture of the hunting.
  But beneath, the Evil Spirits
Lay in ambush, waiting for him,
Broke the treacherous ice beneath him,

Dragged him downward to the bottom,
Buried in the sand his body.
Unktahee, the god of water,
He the god of the Dacotahs,
Drowned him in the deep abysses
Of the lake of Gitche Gumee.

From the headlands Hiawatha
Sent forth such a wail of anguish,
Such a fearful lamentation,
That the bison paused to listen,
And the wolves howled from the prairies,
And the thunder in the distance
Starting answered " Baim-wawa ! "

Then his face with black he painted,
With his robe his head he covered,
In his wigwam sat lamenting,
Seven long weeks he sat lamenting,
Uttering still this moan of sorrow : —

" He is dead, the sweet musician !
He the sweetest of all singers !
He has gone from us forever,
He has moved a little nearer
To the Master of all music,
To the Master of all singing !
O my brother, Chibiabos ! "

And the melancholy fir-trees
Waved their dark green fans above him,

Waved their purple cones above him,
Sighing with him to console him,
Mingling with his lamentation
Their complaining, their lamenting.
    Came the Spring, and all the forest
Looked in vain for Chibiabos;
Sighed the rivulet, Sebowisha,
Sighed the rushes in the meadow.
    From the tree-tops sang the bluebird,
Sang the bluebird, the Owaissa,
" Chibiabos ! Chibiabos !
He is dead, the sweet musician ! "
    From the wigwam sang the robin,
Sang the robin, the Opechee,
" Chibiabos ! Chibiabos !
He is dead, the sweetest singer ! "
    And at night through all the forest
Went the whippoorwill complaining,
Wailing went the Wawonaissa,
" Chibiabos ! Chibiabos !
He is dead, the sweet musician !
He the sweetest of all singers ! "
    Then the medicine-men, the Medas,
The magicians, the Wabenos,
And the Jossakeeds, the Prophets,
Came to visit Hiawatha ;
Built a Sacred Lodge beside him,

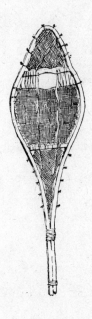

To appease him, to console him,
Walked in silent, grave procession,
Bearing each a pouch of healing,
Skin of beaver, lynx, or otter,
Filled with magic roots and simples,
Filled with very potent medicines.

When he heard their steps approaching,
Hiawatha ceased lamenting,
Called no more on Chibiabos;
Naught he questioned, naught he answered,
But his mournful head uncovered,
From his face the mourning colors
Washed he slowly and in silence,
Slowly and in silence followed
Onward to the Sacred Wigwam.

There a magic drink they gave him,
Made of Nahma-wusk, the spearmint,
And Wabeno-wusk, the yarrow,
Roots of power, and herbs of healing;
Beat their drums, and shook their rattles;
Chanted singly and in chorus,
Mystic songs like these, they chanted.

"I myself, myself! behold me!
'T is the great Gray Eagle talking;
Come, ye white crows, come and hear him!
The loud-speaking thunder helps me;
All the unseen spirits help me;

I can hear their voices calling,
All around the sky I hear them!
I can blow you strong, my brother,
I can heal you, Hiawatha!"
  "Hi-au-ha!" replied the chorus,
"Way-ha-way!" the mystic chorus.

  "Friends of mine are all the serpents!
Hear me shake my skin of hen-hawk!
Mahng, the white loon, I can kill him;
I can shoot your heart and kill it!
I can blow you strong, my brother,
I can heal you, Hiawatha!"
  "Hi-au-ha!" replied the chorus,
"Way-ha-way!" the mystic chorus.

  "I myself, myself! the prophet!
When I speak the wigwam trembles,
Shakes the Sacred Lodge with terror,
Hands unseen begin to shake it!
When I walk, the sky I tread on
Bends and makes a noise beneath me!
I can blow you strong, my brother!
Rise and speak, O Hiawatha!"
  "Hi-au-ha!" replied the chorus,
"Way-ha-way!" the mystic chorus.

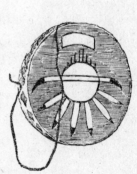

  Then they shook their medicine-pouches
O'er the head of Hiawatha,
Danced their medicine-dance around him;

And upstarting wild and haggard,
Like a man from dreams awakened,
He was healed of all his madness.
As the clouds are swept from heaven,
Straightway from his brain departed
All his moody melancholy ;
As the ice is swept from rivers,
Straightway from his heart departed
All his sorrow and affliction.

Then they summoned Chibiabos
From his grave beneath the waters,
From the sands of Gitche Gumee
Summoned Hiawatha's brother.
And so mighty was the magic
Of that cry and invocation,
That he heard it as he lay there
Underneath the Big-Sea-Water ;
From the sand he rose and listened,
Heard the music and the singing,
Came, obedient to the summons,
To the doorway of the wigwam,
But to enter they forbade him.

Through a chink a coal they gave him,
Through the door a burning fire-brand ;
Ruler in the Land of Spirits,
Ruler o'er the dead, they made him,
Telling him a fire to kindle

" I can blow you strong, my brother,

I can heal you, Hiawatha!"

For all those that died thereafter,
Camp-fires for their night encampments
On their solitary journey
To the kingdom of Ponemah,
To the land of the Hereafter.

From the village of his childhood,
From the homes of those who knew him,
Passing silent through the forest,
Like a smoke-wreath wafted sideways,
Slowly vanished Chibiabos!
Where he passed, the branches moved not,
Where he trod, the grasses bent not,
And the fallen leaves of last year
Made no sound beneath his footsteps.

Four whole days he journeyed onward
Down the pathway of the dead men ;
On the dead-man's strawberry feasted,
Crossed the melancholy river,
On the swinging log he crossed it,
Came unto the Lake of Silver,
In the Stone Canoe was carried
To the Islands of the Blessed,
To the land of ghosts and shadows.

On that journey, moving slowly,
Many weary spirits saw he,
Panting under heavy burdens,
Laden with war-clubs, bows and arrows,

Robes of fur, and pots and kettles,
And with food that friends had given
For that solitary journey.
   " Ay ! why do the living," said they,
" Lay such heavy burdens on us !
Better were it to go naked,
Better were it to go fasting,
Than to bear such heavy burdens
On our long and weary journey ! "
   Forth then issued Hiawatha,
Wandered eastward, wandered westward,
Teaching men the use of simples
And the antidotes for poisons,
And the cure of all diseases.
Thus was first made known to mortals
All the mystery of Medamin,
All the sacred art of healing.

XVI

Pau-Puk-Keewis

You shall hear how Pau-Puk-Keewis
He, the handsome Yenadizze,
Whom the people called the Storm-Fool,
Vexed the village with disturbance;
You shall hear of all his mischief,
And his flight from Hiawatha,
And his wondrous transmigrations,
And the end of his adventures.
  On the shores of Gitche Gumee,
On the dunes of Nagow Wudjoo,
By the shining Big-Sea-Water
Stood the lodge of Pau-Puk-Keewis.

It was he who in his frenzy
Whirled these drifting sands together,
On the dunes of Nagow Wudjoo,
When, among the guests assembled,
He so merrily and madly
Danced at Hiawatha's wedding,
Danced the Beggar's Dance to please them.

Now, in search of new adventures,
From his lodge went Pau-Puk-Keewis,
Came with speed into the village,
Found the young men all assembled
In the lodge of old Iagoo,
Listening to his monstrous stories,
To his wonderful adventures.

He was telling them the story
Of Ojeeg, the Summer-Maker,
How he made a hole in heaven,
How he climbed up into heaven,
And let out the summer-weather,
The perpetual, pleasant Summer;
How the Otter first essayed it;
How the Beaver, Lynx, and Badger
Tried in turn the great achievement,
From the summit of the mountain
Smote their fists against the heavens,
Smote against the sky their foreheads,
Cracked the sky, but could not break it;

How the Wolverine, uprising,
Made him ready for the encounter,
Bent his knees down, like a squirrel,
Drew his arms back, like a cricket.

"Once he leaped," said old Iagoo,
"Once he leaped, and lo! above him
Bent the sky, as ice in rivers
When the waters rise beneath it;
Twice he leaped, and lo! above him
Cracked the sky, as ice in rivers
When the freshet is at highest!
Thrice he leaped, and lo! above him
Broke the shattered sky asunder,
And he disappeared within it,
And Ojeeg, the Fisher Weasel,
With a bound went in behind him!"

"Hark you!" shouted Pau-Puk-Keewis
As he entered at the doorway;
"I am tired of all this talking,
Tired of old Iagoo's stories,
Tired of Hiawatha's wisdom.
Here is something to amuse you,
Better than this endless talking."

Then from out his pouch of wolf-skin
Forth he drew, with solemn manner,
All the game of Bowl and Counters,
Pugasaing, with thirteen pieces.

White on one side were they painted,
And vermilion on the other ;
Two Kenabeeks or great serpents,
Two Ininewug or wedge-men,
One great war-club, Pugamaugun,
And one slender fish, the Keego,
Four round pieces, Ozawabeeks,
And three Sheshebwug or ducklings.
All were made of bone and painted,
All except the Ozawabeeks ;
These were brass, on one side burnished,
And were black upon the other.

In a wooden bowl he placed them,
Shook and jostled them together,
Threw them on the ground before him.
Thus exclaiming and explaining :
" Red side up are all the pieces,
And one great Kenabeek standing
On the bright side of a brass piece,
On a burnished Ozawabeek ;
Thirteen tens and eight are counted."

Then again he shook the pieces,
Shook and jostled them together,
Threw them on the ground before him,
Still exclaiming and explaining :
" White are both the great Kenabeeks,
White the Ininewug, the wedge-men,

Red are all the other pieces ;
Five tens and an eight are counted."
  Thus he taught the game of hazard,
Thus displayed it and explained it,
Running through its various chances,
Various changes, various meanings :
Twenty curious eyes stared at him.
Full of eagerness stared at him.
  " Many games," said old Iagoo,
" Many games of skill and hazard
Have I seen in different nations,
Have I played in different countries.
He who plays with old Iagoo
Must have very nimble fingers ;
Though you think yourself so skilful
I can beat you, Pau-Puk-Keewis,
I can even give you lessons
In your game of Bowl and Counters ! '
  So they sat and played together,
All the old men and the young men,
Played for dresses, weapons, wampum,
Played till midnight, played till morning,
Played until the Yenadizze,
Till the cunning Pau-Puk-Keewis,
Of their treasures had despoiled them,
Of the best of all their dresses,
Shirts of deer-skin, robes of ermine,

Belts of wampum, crests of feathers,
Warlike weapons, pipes and pouches.
Twenty eyes glared wildly at him,
Like the eyes of wolves glared at him.
Said the lucky Pau-Puk-Keewis :
"In my wigwam I am lonely,
In my wanderings and adventures
I have need of a companion,
Fain would have a Meshinauwa,
An attendant and pipe-bearer.
I will venture all these winnings,
All these garments heaped about me,
All this wampum, all these feathers,
On a single throw will venture
All against the young man yonder ! "
'T was a youth of sixteen summers,
'T was a nephew of Iagoo ;
Face-in-a-Mist, the people called him.
    As the fire burns in a pipe-head
Dusky red beneath the ashes,
So beneath his shaggy eyebrows
Glowed the eyes of old Iagoo.
"Ugh ! " he answered very fiercely ;
"Ugh ! " they answered all and each one.
    Seized the wooden bowl the old man,
Closely in his bony fingers
Clutched the fatal bowl, Onagon,

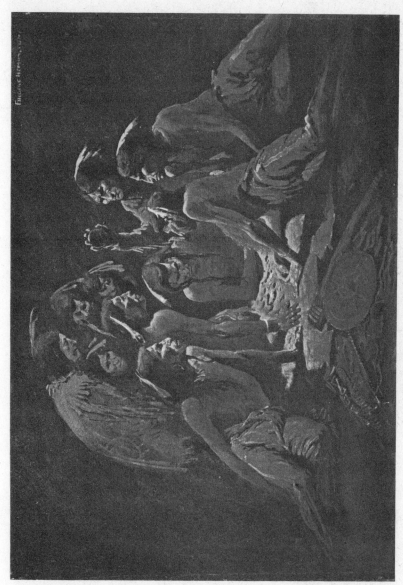

All the old men and the young men, · · · ·
Played till midnight, played till morning

Shook it fiercely and with fury,
Made the pieces ring together
As he threw them down before him.

   Red were both the great Kenabeeks,
Red the Ininewug, the wedge-men,
Red the Sheshebwug, the ducklings,
Black the four brass Ozawabeeks,
White alone the fish, the Keego;
Only five the pieces counted!

   Then the smiling Pau-Puk-Keewis
Shook the bowl and threw the pieces;
Lightly in the air he tossed them,
And they fell about him scattered;
Dark and bright the Ozawabeeks,
Red and white the other pieces,
And upright among the others
One Ininewug was standing,
Even as crafty Pau-Puk-Keewis
Stood alone among the players,
Saying, " Five tens! mine the game is!"

   Twenty eyes glared at him fiercely,
Like the eyes of wolves glared at him,
As he turned and left the wigwam,
Followed by his Meshinauwa,
By the nephew of Iagoo,
By the tall and graceful stripling,
Bearing in his arms the winnings,

Shirts of deer-skin, robes of ermine,
Belts of wampum, pipes and weapons.
"Carry them," said Pau-Puk-Keewis,
Pointing with his fan of feathers,
"To my wigwam far to eastward,
On the dunes of Nagow Wudjoo!"
Hot and red with smoke and gambling
Were the eyes of Pau-Puk-Keewis
As he came forth to the freshness
Of the pleasant Summer morning.

All the birds were singing gayly,
All the streamlets flowing swiftly,
And the heart of Pau-Puk-Keewis
Sang with pleasure as the birds sing,
Beat with triumph like the streamlets,
As he wandered through the village,
In the early gray of morning,
With his fan of turkey-feathers,

With his plumes and tufts of swan's down,
Till he reached the farthest wigwam,
Reached the lodge of Hiawatha.
Silent was it and deserted;
No one met him at the doorway,
No one came to bid him welcome;
But the birds were singing round it,
In and out and round the doorway,
Hopping, singing, fluttering, feeding,
And aloft upon the ridge-pole

Kahgahgee, the King of Ravens,
Sat with fiery eyes, and, screaming,
Flapped his wings at Pau-Puk-Keewis.

 " All are gone ! the lodge is empty ! "
Thus it was spake Pau-Puk-Keewis,
In his heart resolving mischief ; —
" Gone is wary Hiawatha,
Gone the silly Laughing Water,
Gone Nokomis, the old woman,
And the lodge is left unguarded ! "

 By the neck he seized the raven,
Whirled it round him like a rattle,
Like a medicine-pouch he shook it,
Strangled Kahgahgee, the raven,
From the ridge-pole of the wigwam
Left its lifeless body hanging,
As an insult to its master,
As a taunt to Hiawatha.

 With a stealthy step he entered,
Round the lodge in wild disorder
Threw the household things about him,
Piled together in confusion
Bowls of wood and earthen kettles,
Robes of buffalo and beaver,
Skins of otter, lynx, and ermine,
As an insult to Nokomis,
As a taunt to Minnehaha.

 Then departed Pau-Puk-Keewis,

Whistling, singing through the forest,
Whistling gayly to the squirrels,
Who from hollow boughs above him
Dropped their acorn-shells upon him,
Singing gayly to the wood birds,
Who from out the leafy darkness
Answered with a song as merry.

Then he climbed the rocky headlands,
Looking o'er the Gitche Gumee,
Perched himself upon their summit,
Waiting full of mirth and mischief
The return of Hiawatha.

Stretched upon his back he lay there;
Far below him plashed the waters,
Plashed and washed the dreamy waters;
Far above him swam the heavens,
Swam the dizzy, dreamy heavens;
Round him hovered, fluttered, rustled,
Hiawatha's mountain chickens,
Flock-wise swept and wheeled about him,
Almost brushed him with their pinions.

And he killed them as he lay there,
Slaughtered them by tens and twenties,
Threw their bodies down the headland,
Threw them on the beach below him,
Till at length Kayoshk, the sea-gull,
Perched upon a crag above them,

Shouted: " It is Pau-Puk-Keewis !
He is slaying us by hundreds !
Send a message to our brother,
Tidings send to Hiawatha ! "

XVII

The Hunting of Pau-Puk-Keewis

Full of wrath was Hiawatha
When he came into the village,
Found the people in confusion,
Heard of all the misdemeanors,
All the malice and the mischief,
Of the cunning Pau-Puk-Keewis.

    Hard his breath came through his nostrils,

Through his teeth he buzzed and muttered
Words of anger and resentment,
Hot and humming, like a hornet.
" I will slay this Pau-Puk-Keewis,
Slay this mischief-maker ! " said he.
" Not so long and wide the world is,
Not so rude and rough the way is,
That my wrath shall not attain him,
That my vengeance shall not reach him ! "
Then in swift pursuit departed
Hiawatha and the hunters
On the trail of Pau-Puk-Keewis,
Through the forest, where he passed it,
To the headlands where he rested ;
But they found not Pau-Puk-Keewis,
Only in the trampled grasses,
In the whortleberry-bushes,
Found the couch where he had rested,
Found the impress of his body.
From the lowlands far beneath them,
From the Muskoday, the meadow,
Pau-Puk-Keewis, turning backward,
Made a gesture of defiance,
Made a gesture of derision ;
And aloud cried Hiawatha,
From the summit of the mountains :
" Not so long and wide the world is,

Not so rude and rough the way is,
But my wrath shall overtake you,
And my vengeance shall attain you!"
   Over rock and over river,
Thorough bush, and brake, and forest,
Ran the cunning Pau-Puk-Keewis;
Like an antelope he bounded,
Till he came unto a streamlet
In the middle of the forest,
To a streamlet still and tranquil,
That had overflowed its margin,
To a dam made by the beavers,
To a pond of quiet water,
Where knee-deep the trees were standing,
Where the water-lilies floated,
Where the rushes waved and whispered.
   On the dam stood Pau-Puk-Keewis,
On the dam of trunks and branches,
Through whose chinks the water spouted,
O'er whose summit flowed the streamlet.
From the bottom rose the beaver,
Looked with two great eyes of wonder,
Eyes that seemed to ask a question,
At the stranger, Pau-Puk-Keewis.
   On the dam stood Pau-Puk-Keewis,
O'er his ankles flowed the streamlet,
Flowed the bright and silvery water,

Thorough bush, and brake, and forest,
Ran the cunning Pau-Puk-Keewis

And he spake unto the beaver,
With a smile he spake in this wise :
   "O my friend Ahmeek, the beaver,
Cool and pleasant is the water ;
Let me dive into the water,
Let me rest there in your lodges ;
Change me, too, into a beaver ! "
   Cautiously replied the beaver,
With reserve he thus made answer :
" Let me first consult the others,
Let me ask the other beavers."
Down he sank into the water,
Heavily sank he, as a stone sinks,
Down among the leaves and branches,
Brown and matted at the bottom.

   On the dam stood Pau-Puk-Keewis,
O'er his ankles flowed the streamlet,
Spouted through the chinks below him,
Dashed upon the stones beneath him,
Spread serene and calm before him,
And the sunshine and the shadows
Fell in flecks and gleams upon him,
Fell in little shining patches,
Through the waving, rustling branches.
   From the bottom rose the beavers,
Silently above the surface
Rose one head and then another,

Till the pond seemed full of beavers,
Full of black and shining faces.

　　To the beavers Pau-Puk-Keewis
Spake entreating, said in this wise:
" Very pleasant is your dwelling,
　O my friends ! and safe from danger ;
　Can you not with all your cunning,
　All your wisdom and contrivance,
　Change me, too, into a beaver ? "

　　" Yes ! " replied Ahmeek, the beaver,
He the King of all the beavers,
" Let yourself slide down among us,
　Down into the tranquil water."

　　Down into the pond among them
Silently sank Pau-Puk-Keewis ;
Black became his shirt of deer-skin,
Black his moccasins and leggings,
In a broad black tail behind him
Spread his fox-tails and his fringes ;
He was changed into a beaver.

　　" Make me large," said Pau-Puk-Keewis,
" Make me large and make me larger,
Larger than the other beavers."
" Yes," the beaver chief responded,
" When our lodge below you enter,
　In our wigwam we will make you
　Ten times larger than the others."

Thus into the clear, brown water
Silently sank Pau-Puk-Keewis :
Found the bottom covered over
With the trunks of trees and branches,
Hoards of food against the winter,
Piles and heaps against the famine ;
Found the lodge with arching doorway,
Leading into spacious chambers.
    Here they made him large and larger,
Made him largest of the beavers,
Ten times larger than the others.
" You shall be our ruler," said they ;
" Chief and King of all the beavers."
    But not long had Pau-Puk-Keewis
Sat in state among the beavers,
When there came a voice of warning
From the watchman at his station
In the water-flags and lilies,
Saying, " Here is Hiawatha !
Hiawatha with his hunters ! "
    Then they heard a cry above them,
Heard a shouting and a tramping,
Heard a crashing and a rushing,
And the water round and o'er them
Sank and sucked away in eddies,
And they knew their dam was broken.
    On the lodge's roof the hunters

Leaped, and broke it all asunder;
Streamed the sunshine through the crevice,
Sprang the beavers through the doorway,
Hid themselves in deeper water,
In the channel of the streamlet;
But the mighty Pau-Puk-Keewis
Could not pass beneath the doorway;
He was puffed with pride and feeding,
He was swollen like a bladder.

Through the roof looked Hiawatha,
Cried aloud, " O Pau-Puk-Keewis!
Vain are all your craft and cunning,
Vain your manifold disguises!
Well I know you, Pau-Puk-Keewis! "
With their clubs they beat and bruised him,
Beat to death poor Pau-Puk-Keewis,
Pounded him as maize is pounded,
Till his skull was crushed to pieces.

Six tall hunters, lithe and limber,
Bore him home on poles and branches,
Bore the body of the beaver;
But the ghost, the Jeebi in him,
Thought and felt as Pau-Puk-Keewis,
Still lived on as Pau-Puk-Keewis.

And it fluttered, strove, and struggled,
Waving hither, waving thither,
As the curtains of a wigwam
Struggle with their thongs of deer-skin,

When the wintry wind is blowing;
Till it drew itself together,
Till it rose up from the body,
Till it took the form and features
Of the cunning Pau-Puk-Keewis
Vanishing into the forest.

But the wary Hiawatha
Saw the figure ere it vanished,
Saw the form of Pau-Puk-Keewis
Glide into the soft blue shadow
Of the pine-trees of the forest;
Toward the squares of white beyond it,
Toward an opening in the forest,
Like a wind it rushed and panted,
Bending all the boughs before it,
And behind it, as the rain comes,
Came the steps of Hiawatha.

To a lake with many islands
Came the breathless Pau-Puk-Keewis,
Where among the water-lilies
Pishnekuh, the brant, were sailing;
Through the tufts of rushes floating,
Steering through the reedy islands.
Now their broad black beaks they lifted,
Now they plunged beneath the water,
Now they darkened in the shadow,
Now they brightened in the sunshine.

"Pishnekuh!" cried Pau-Puk-Keewis,

"Pishnekuh ! my brothers !" said he,
"Change me to a brant with plumage,
   With a shining neck and feathers,
   Make me large, and make me larger,
   Ten times larger than the others."
      Straightway to a brant they changed him,
   With two huge and dusky pinions,
   With a bosom smooth and rounded,
   With a bill like two great paddles,
   Made him larger than the others,
   Ten times larger than the largest,
   Just as, shouting from the forest,
   On the shore stood Hiawatha.

      Up they rose with cry and clamor,
   With a whir and beat of pinions,
   Rose up from the reedy islands,
   From the water-flags and lilies.
   And they said to Pau-Puk-Keewis :
"In your flying, look not downward,
   Take good heed, and look not downward,
   Lest some strange mischance should happen,
   Lest some great mishap befall you ! "
      Fast and far they fled to northward,
   Fast and far through mist and sunshine,
   Fed among the moors and fen-lands,
   Slept among the reeds and rushes.
      On the morrow as they journeyed,

Buoyed and lifted by the South-wind,
Wafted onward by the South-wind,
Blowing fresh and strong behind them,
Rose a sound of human voices,
Rose a clamor from beneath them,
From the lodges of a village,
From the people miles beneath them.

For the people of the village
Saw the flock of brant with wonder,
Saw the wings of Pau-Puk-Keewis
Flapping far up in the ether,
Broader than two doorway curtains.

Pau-Puk-Keewis heard the shouting,
Knew the voice of Hiawatha,
Knew the outcry of Iagoo,
And forgetful of the warning,
Drew his neck in, and looked downward,
And the wind that blew behind him
Caught his mighty fan of feathers,
Sent him wheeling, whirling downward!

All in vain did Pau-Puk-Keewis
Struggle to regain his balance!
Whirling round and round and downward,
He beheld in turn the village
And in turn the flock above him,
Saw the village coming nearer,
And the flock receding farther,

Heard the voices growing louder,
Heard the shouting and the laughter;
Saw no more the flock above him,
Only saw the earth beneath him;
Dead out of the empty heaven,
Dead among the shouting people,
With a heavy sound and sullen,
Fell the brant with broken pinions.

But his soul, his ghost, his shadow,
Still survived as Pau-Puk-Keewis,
Took again the form and features
Of the handsome Yenadizze,
And again went rushing onward,
Followed fast by Hiawatha,
Crying: "Not so wide the world is,
Not so long and rough the way is,
But my wrath shall overtake you,
But my vengeance shall attain you!"

And so near he came, so near him,
That his hand was stretched to seize him,
His right hand to seize and hold him,
When the cunning Pau-Puk-Keewis
Whirled and spun about in circles,
Fanned the air into a whirlwind,
Danced the dust and leaves about him,
And amid the whirling eddies
Sprang into a hollow oak-tree,

Changed himself into a serpent,
Gliding out through root and rubbish.

With his right hand Hiawatha
Smote amain the hollow oak-tree,
Rent it into shreds and splinters,
Left it lying there in fragments.
But in vain ; for Pau-Puk-Keewis,
Once again in human figure,
Full in sight ran on before him,
Sped away in gust and whirlwind,
On the shores of Gitche Gumee,
Westward by the Big-Sea-Water,
Came unto the rocky headlands,
To the Pictured Rocks of sandstone,
Looking over lake and landscape.

And the Old Man of the Mountain,
He the Manito of Mountains,
Opened wide his rocky doorways,
Opened wide his deep abysses,
Giving Pau-Puk-Keewis shelter
In his caverns dark and dreary,
Bidding Pau-Puk-Keewis welcome
To his gloomy lodge of sandstone.

There without stood Hiawatha,
Found the doorways closed against him,
With his mittens, Minjekahwun,
Smote great caverns in the sandstone,

Cried aloud in tones of thunder,
"Open! I am Hiawatha!"
But the Old Man of the Mountain
Opened not, and made no answer
From the silent crags of sandstone,
From the gloomy rock abysses.

Then he raised his hands to heaven,
Called imploring on the tempest,
Called Waywassimo, the lightning,
And the thunder, Annemeekee;
And they came with night and darkness,
Sweeping down the Big-Sea-Water
From the distant Thunder Mountains;
And the trembling Pau-Puk-Keewis
Heard the footsteps of the thunder,
Saw the red eyes of the lightning,
Was afraid, and crouched and trembled.

Then Waywassimo, the lightning,
Smote the doorways of the caverns,
With his war-club smote the doorways,
Smote the jutting crags of sandstone,
And the thunder, Annemeekee,
Shouted down into the caverns,
Saying, "Where is Pau-Puk-Keewis!"
And the crags fell, and beneath them
Dead among the rocky ruins
Lay the cunning Pau-Puk-Keewis,

Lay the handsome Yenadizze,
Slain in his own human figure.

Ended were his wild adventures,
Ended were his tricks and gambols,
Ended all his craft and cunning,
Ended all his mischief-making,
All his gambling and his dancing,
All his wooing of the maidens.

Then the noble Hiawatha
Took his soul, his ghost, his shadow,
Spake and said : " O Pau-Puk-Keewis,
Never more in human figure
Shall you search for new adventures ;
Never more with jest and laughter
Dance the dust and leaves in whirlwinds ;
But above there in the heavens
You shall soar and sail in circles ;
I will change you to an eagle,
To Keneu, the great war-eagle,
Chief of all the fowls with feathers,
Chief of Hiawatha's chickens."

And the name of Pau-Puk-Keewis
Lingers still among the people,
Lingers still among the singers,
And among the story-tellers ;
And in Winter, when the snow-flakes
Whirl in eddies round the lodges,

When the wind in gusty tumult
O'er the smoke-flue pipes and whistles,
"There," they cry, "comes Pau-Puk-Keewis,
He is dancing through the village,
He is gathering in his harvest!"

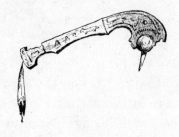

XVIII

The Death of Kwasind

FAR and wide among the nations
Spread the name and fame of Kwasind;
No man dared to strive with Kwasind,
No man could compete with Kwasind.
But the mischievous Puk-Wudjies,
They the envious Little People,
They the fairies and the pygmies,
Plotted and conspired against him.

"If this hateful Kwasind," said they,
"If this great, outrageous fellow
Goes on thus a little longer,
Tearing everything he touches,
Rending everything to pieces,
Filling all the world with wonder,
What becomes of the Puk-Wudjies?
Who will care for the Puk-Wudjies?
He will tread us down like mushrooms,
Drive us all into the water,
Give our bodies to be eaten
By the wicked Nee-ba-naw-baigs,
By the Spirits of the water!"
So the angry Little People
All conspired against the Strong Man,
All conspired to murder Kwasind,
Yes, to rid the world of Kwasind,
The audacious, overbearing,
Heartless, haughty, dangerous Kwasind!

  Now this wondrous strength of Kwasind
In his crown alone was seated;
In his crown too was his weakness;
There alone could he be wounded,
Nowhere else could weapon pierce him,
Nowhere else could weapon harm him.
  Even there the only weapon
That could wound him, that could slay him,

Was the seed-cone of the pine-tree,
Was the blue cone of the fir-tree.
This was Kwasind's fatal secret,
Known to no man among mortals;
But the cunning Little People,
The Puk-Wudjies, knew the secret,
Knew the only way to kill him.

So they gathered cones together,
Gathered seed-cones of the pine-tree,
Gathered blue cones of the fir-tree,
In the woods by Taquamenaw,
Brought them to the river's margin,
Heaped them in great piles together,
Where the red rocks from the margin
Jutting overhang the river.
There they lay in wait for Kwasind,
The malicious Little People.

'T was an afternoon in Summer;
Very hot and still the air was,
Very smooth the gliding river,
Motionless the sleeping shadows:
Insects glistened in the sunshine,
Insects skated on the water,
Filled the drowsy air with buzzing,
With a far resounding war-cry.

Down the river came the Strong Man,
In his birch canoe came Kwasind,

Floating slowly down the current
Of the sluggish Taquamenaw,
Very languid with the weather,
Very sleepy with the silence.

From the overhanging branches,
From the tassels of the birch-trees,
Soft the Spirit of Sleep descended;
By his airy hosts surrounded,
His invisible attendants,
Came the Spirit of Sleep, Nepahwin;
Like the burnished Dush-kwo-ne-she,
Like a dragon-fly, he hovered
O'er the drowsy head of Kwasind.

To his ear there came a murmur
As of waves upon a sea-shore,
As of far-off tumbling waters,
As of winds among the pine-trees;
And he felt upon his forehead
Blows of little airy war-clubs,
Wielded by the slumbrous legions
Of the Spirit of Sleep, Nepahwin,
As of some one breathing on him.

At the first blow of their war-clubs,
Fell a drowsiness on Kwasind;
At the second blow they smote him,
Motionless his paddle rested;
At the third, before his vision

Sideways fell into the river,
Plunged beneath the sluggish water

Reeled the landscape into darkness,
Very sound asleep was Kwasind.

So he floated down the river,
Like a blind man seated upright,
Floated down the Taquamenaw,
Underneath the trembling birch-trees,
Underneath the wooded headlands,
Underneath the war encampment
Of the pygmies, the Puk-Wudjies.

There they stood, all armed and waiting,
Hurled the pine-cones down upon him,
Struck him on his brawny shoulders,
On his crown defenceless struck him.
" Death to Kwasind ! " was the sudden
War-cry of the Little People.

And he sideways swayed and tumbled,
Sideways fell into the river,
Plunged beneath the sluggish water
Headlong, as an otter plunges ;
And the birch canoe, abandoned,
Drifted empty down the river,
Bottom upward swerved and drifted :
Nothing more was seen of Kwasind.

But the memory of the Strong Man
Lingered long among the people,
And whenever through the forest
Raged and roared the wintry tempest,

And the branches, tossed and troubled,
Creaked and groaned and split asunder,
"Kwasind!" cried they; "that is Kwasind!
He is gathering in his fire-wood!"

XIX

The Ghosts

NEVER stoops the soaring vulture
On his quarry in the desert,
On the sick or wounded bison,
But another vulture, watching
From his high aerial look-out,
Sees the downward plunge, and follows;
And a third pursues the second,
Coming from the invisible ether,

First a speck, and then a vulture,
Till the air is dark with pinions.
    So disasters come not singly;
But as if they watched and waited,
Scanning one another's motions,
When the first descends, the others
Follow, follow, gathering flock-wise
Round their victim, sick and wounded,
First a shadow, then a sorrow,
Till the air is dark with anguish.
    Now, o'er all the dreary North-land,
Mighty Peboan, the Winter,
Breathing on the lakes and rivers,
Into stone had changed their waters.
From his hair he shook the snow-flakes,
Till the plains were strewn with whiteness,
One uninterrupted level,
As if, stooping, the Creator
With his hand had smoothed them over.
    Through the forest, wide and wailing,
Roamed the hunter on his snow-shoes;
In the village worked the women,

Pounded maize, or dressed the deer-skin;
And the young men played together
On the ice the noisy ball-play,
On the plain the dance of snow-shoes.
    One dark evening, after sundown,

In her wigwam Laughing Water
Sat with old Nokomis, waiting
For the steps of Hiawatha
Homeward from the hunt returning.

On their faces gleamed the fire-light,
Painting them with streaks of crimson,
In the eyes of old Nokomis
Glimmered like the watery moonlight,
In the eyes of Laughing Water
Glistened like the sun in water ;
And behind them crouched their shadows
In the corners of the wigwam,
And the smoke in wreaths above them
Climbed and crowded through the smoke-flue.

Then the curtain of the doorway
From without was slowly lifted ;
Brighter glowed the fire a moment,
And a moment swerved the smoke-wreath,
As two women entered softly,
Passed the doorway uninvited,
Without word of salutation,
Without sign of recognition,
Sat down in the farthest corner,
Crouching low among the shadows.

From their aspect and their garments,
Strangers seemed they in the village ;
Very pale and haggard were they,

As they sat there sad and silent,
Trembling, cowering with the shadows.

Was it the wind above the smoke-flue,
Muttering down into the wigwam?
Was it the owl, the Koko-koho,
Hooting from the dismal forest?
Sure a voice said in the silence:
"These are corpses clad in garments,
These are ghosts that come to haunt you,
From the kingdom of Ponemah,
From the land of the Hereafter!"

Homeward now came Hiawatha
From his hunting in the forest,
With the snow upon his tresses,
And the red deer on his shoulders.
At the feet of Laughing Water
Down he threw his lifeless burden;
Nobler, handsomer she thought him,
Than when first he came to woo her,
First threw down the deer before her,
As a token of his wishes,
As a promise of the future.

Then he turned and saw the strangers,
Cowering, crouching with the shadows;
Said within himself, "Who are they?
What strange guests has Minnehaha?"
But he questioned not the strangers,

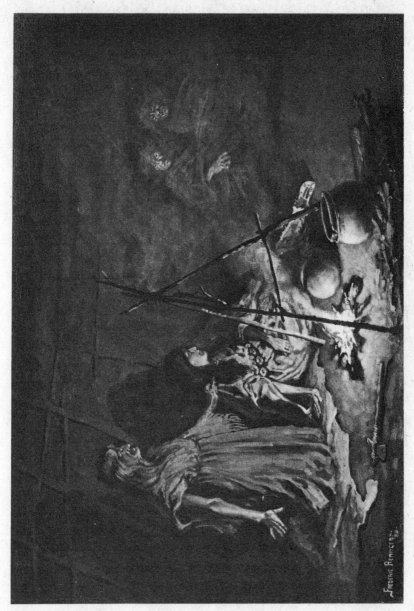

Sat down in the farthest corner,
Crouching low among the shadows

Only spake to bid them welcome
To his lodge, his food, his fireside.

When the evening meal was ready,
And the deer had been divided,
Both the pallid guests, the strangers,
Springing from among the shadows,
Seized upon the choicest portions,
Seized the white fat of the roebuck,
Set apart for Laughing Water,
For the wife of Hiawatha ;
Without asking, without thanking,
Eagerly devoured the morsels,
Flitted back among the shadows
In the corner of the wigwam.

Not a word spake Hiawatha,
Not a motion made Nokomis,
Not a gesture Laughing Water ;
Not a change came o'er their features ;
Only Minnehaha softly
Whispered, saying, " They are famished ;
Let them do what best delights them ;
Let them eat, for they are famished."

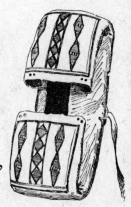

Many a daylight dawned and darkened,
Many a night shook off the daylight
As the pine shakes off the snow-flakes
From the midnight of its branches ;
Day by day the guests unmoving

Sat there silent in the wigwam ;
But by night, in storm or starlight,
Forth they went into the forest,
Bringing fire-wood to the wigwam,
Bringing pine-cones for the burning,
Always sad and always silent.

   And whenever Hiawatha
Came from fishing or from hunting,
When the evening meal was ready,
And the food had been divided,
Gliding from their darksome corner,
Came the pallid guests, the strangers,
Seized upon the choicest portions
Set aside for Laughing Water,
And without rebuke or question
Flitted back among the shadows.
   Never once had Hiawatha
By a word or look reproved them ;
Never once had old Nokomis
Made a gesture of impatience ;
Never once had Laughing Water
Shown resentment at the outrage.
All had they endured in silence,
That the rights of guest and stranger,
That the virtue of free-giving,
By a look might not be lessened,
By a word might not be broken.
   Once at midnight Hiawatha,

Ever wakeful, ever watchful,
In the wigwam, dimly lighted
By the brands that still were burning,
By the glimmering, flickering fire-light,
Heard a sighing, oft repeated,
Heard a sobbing, as of sorrow.

    From his couch rose Hiawatha,
From his shaggy hides of bison,
Pushed aside the deer-skin curtain,
Saw the pallid guests, the shadows,
Sitting upright on their couches,
Weeping in the silent midnight.

    And he said: "O guests! why is it
That your hearts are so afflicted,
That you sob so in the midnight?
Has perchance the old Nokomis,
Has my wife, my Minnehaha,
Wronged or grieved you by unkindness,
Failed in hospitable duties?"

    Then the shadows ceased from weeping,
Ceased from sobbing and lamenting,
And they said, with gentle voices:

"We are ghosts of the departed,
Souls of those who once were with you.
From the realms of Chibiabos
Hither have we come to try you,
Hither have we come to warn you.

    "Cries of grief and lamentation

Reach us in the Blessed Islands ;
Cries of anguish from the living,
Calling back their friends departed,
Sadden us with useless sorrow.
Therefore have we come to try you ;
No one knows us, no one heeds us.
We are but a burden to you,
And we see that the departed
Have no place among the living.

"Think of this, O Hiawatha!
Speak of it to all the people,
That henceforward and forever
They no more with lamentations
Sadden the souls of the departed
In the Islands of the Blessed.

"Do not lay such heavy burdens
In the graves of those you bury,
Not such weight of furs and wampum,
Not such weight of pots and kettles,
For the spirits faint beneath them.
Only give them·food to carry,
Only give them fire to light them.

"Four days is the spirit's journey
To the land of ghosts and shadows,
Four its lonely night encampments ;
Four times must their fires be lighted.
Therefore, when the dead are buried,

Let a fire, as night approaches,
Four times on the grave be kindled,
That the soul upon its journey
May not lack the cheerful fire-light,
May not grope about in darkness.
  "Farewell, noble Hiawatha!
We have put you to the trial,
To the proof have put your patience,
By the insult of our presence,
By the outrage of our actions.
We have found you great and noble.
Fail not in the greater trial,
Faint not in the harder struggle."
  When they ceased, a sudden darkness

Fell and filled the silent wigwam.
Hiawatha heard a rustle
As of garments trailing by him,
Heard the curtain of the doorway
Lifted by a hand he saw not,
Felt the cold breath of the night air,
For a moment saw the star-light;
But he saw the ghosts no longer,
Saw no more the wandering spirits
From the kingdom of Ponemah,
From the land of the Hereafter.

XX

The Famine

Oh the long and dreary Winter!
Oh the cold and cruel Winter!
Ever thicker, thicker, thicker
Froze the ice on lake and river,
Ever deeper, deeper, deeper
Fell the snow o'er all the landscape,
Fell the covering snow, and drifted
Through the forest, round the village.

Hardly from his buried wigwam
Could the hunter force a passage;
With his mittens and his snow-shoes
Vainly walked he through the forest,

Sought for bird or beast and found none,
Saw no track of deer or rabbit,
In the snow beheld no footprints,
In the ghastly, gleaming forest
Fell, and could not rise from weakness,
Perished there from cold and hunger.

   Oh the famine and the fever!
Oh the wasting of the famine!
Oh the blasting of the fever!
Oh the wailing of the children!
Oh the anguish of the women!

   All the earth was sick and famished;
Hungry was the air around them,
Hungry was the sky above them,
And the hungry stars in heaven
Like the eyes of wolves glared at them!

   Into Hiawatha's wigwam
Came two other guests, as silent
As the ghosts were, and as gloomy,
Waited not to be invited,
Did not parley at the doorway,
Sat there without word of welcome
In the seat of Laughing Water;
Looked with haggard eyes and hollow
At the face of Laughing Water.

   And the foremost said: "Behold me!
I am Famine, Bukadawin!"

And the other said: "Behold me!
I am Fever, Ahkosewin!"
    And the lovely Minnehaha
Shuddered as they looked upon her,
Shuddered at the words they uttered,
Lay down on her bed in silence,
Hid her face, but made no answer;
Lay there trembling, freezing, burning
At the looks they cast upon her,
At the fearful words they uttered.
    Forth into the empty forest
Rushed the maddened Hiawatha;
In his heart was deadly sorrow,
In his face a stony firmness;
On his brow the sweat of anguish
Started, but it froze and fell not.
    Wrapped in furs and armed for hunting,
With his mighty bow of ash-tree,
With his quiver full of arrows,
With his mittens, Minjekahwun,
Into the vast and vacant forest
On his snow-shoes strode he forward.
    "Gitche Manito, the Mighty!"
Cried he with his face uplifted
In that bitter hour of anguish,
"Give your children food, O father!
Give us food, or we must perish!"

Give me food for Minnehaha,
For my dying Minnehaha!"
   Through the far-resounding forest,
Through the forest vast and vacant
Rang that cry of desolation,
But there came no other answer
Than the echo of his crying,
Than the echo of the woodlands,
" Minnehaha! Minnehaha!"
   All day long roved Hiawatha
In that melancholy forest,
Through the shadow of whose thickets
In the pleasant days of Summer,
Of that ne'er forgotten Summer,
He had brought his young wife homeward
From the land of the Dacotahs;
When the birds sang in the thickets,
And the streamlets laughed and glistened,
And the air was full of fragrance,
And the lovely Laughing Water
Said with voice that did not tremble,
" I will follow you, my husband!"
   In the wigwam with Nokomis,
With those gloomy guests, that watched her,
With the Famine and the Fever,
She was lying, the Beloved,
She the dying Minnehaha.

" Hark ! " she said ; " I hear a rushing,
Hear a roaring and a rushing,
Hear the Falls of Minnehaha
Calling to me from a distance ! "
" No, my child ! " said old Nokomis,
" 'T is the night-wind in the pine-trees ! "
" Look ! " she said ; " I see my father
Standing lonely at his doorway,
Beckoning to me from his wigwam
In the land of the Dacotahs ! "
" No, my child ! " said old Nokomis,
" 'T is the smoke, that waves and beckons ! "
" Ah ! " said she, " the eyes of Pauguk
Glare upon me in the darkness,
I can feel his icy fingers
Clasping mine amid the darkness !
Hiawatha ! Hiawatha ! "

And the desolate Hiawatha,
Far away amid the forest,
Miles away among the mountains,
Heard that sudden cry of anguish,
Heard the voice of Minnehaha
Calling to him in the darkness,
" Hiawatha ! Hiawatha ! "
Over snow-fields waste and pathless,
Under snow-encumbered branches,
Homeward hurried Hiawatha,

Then he sat down, still and speechless, ...
At the feet of Laughing Water

Empty-handed, heavy-hearted,
Heard Nokomis moaning, wailing:
" Wahonowin! Wahonowin!
Would that I had perished for you,
Would that I were dead as you are!
Wahonowin! Wahonowin!"

And he rushed into the wigwam,
Saw the old Nokomis slowly
Rocking to and fro and moaning,
Saw his lovely Minnehaha
Lying dead and cold before him,
And his bursting heart within him
Uttered such a cry of anguish,
That the forest moaned and shuddered,
That the very stars in heaven
Shook and trembled with his anguish.

Then he sat down, still and speechless,
On the bed of Minnehaha,
At the feet of Laughing Water,
At those willing feet, that never
More would lightly run to meet him,
Never more would lightly follow.

With both hands his face he covered,
Seven long days and nights he sat there,
As if in a swoon he sat there,
Speechless, motionless, unconscious
Of the daylight or the darkness.

Then they buried Minnehaha;
In the snow a grave they made her,
In the forest deep and darksome,
Underneath the moaning hemlocks;
Clothed her in her richest garments,
Wrapped her in her robes of ermine,
Covered her with snow, like ermine;
Thus they buried Minnehaha.

And at night a fire was lighted,
On her grave four times was kindled,
For her soul upon its journey
To the Islands of the Blessed.
From his doorway Hiawatha
Saw it burning in the forest,
Lighting up the gloomy hemlocks;
From his sleepless bed uprising,
From the bed of Minnehaha,
Stood and watched it at the doorway,
That it might not be extinguished,
Might not leave her in the darkness.

"Farewell!" said he, "Minnehaha!
Farewell, O my Laughing Water!
All my heart is buried with you,
All my thoughts go onward with you!
Come not back again to labor,
Come not back again to suffer,
Where the Famine and the Fever

Wear the heart and waste the body.
Soon my task will be completed,
Soon your footsteps I shall follow
To the Islands of the Blessed,
To the Kingdom of Ponemah,
To the land of the Hereafter!"

XXI

The White-Man's Foot

In his lodge beside a river,
Close beside a frozen river,
Sat an old man, sad and lonely.
White his hair was as a snow-drift;
Dull and low his fire was burning,
And the old man shook and trembled,
Folded in his Waubewyon,
In his tattered white-skin-wrapper,
Hearing nothing but the tempest
As it roared along the forest,
Seeing nothing but the snow-storm,
As it whirled and hissed and drifted.

   All the coals were white with ashes,
And the fire was slowly dying,
As a young man, walking lightly,

At the open doorway entered.
Red with blood of youth his cheeks were,
Soft his eyes, as stars in Spring-time,
Bound his forehead was with grasses ;
Bound and plumed with scented grasses,
On his lips a smile of beauty,
Filling all the lodge with sunshine,
In his hand a bunch of blossoms
Filling all the lodge with sweetness.

    " Ah, my son ! " exclaimed the old man,
" Happy are my eyes to see you.
Sit here on the mat beside me,
Sit here by the dying embers,
Let us pass the night together.
Tell me of your strange adventures,
Of the lands where you have travelled ;
I will tell you of my prowess,
Of my many deeds of wonder."

    From his pouch he drew his peace-pipe,
Very old and strangely fashioned ;
Made of red stone was the pipe-head,
And the stem a reed with feathers ;
Filled the pipe with bark of willow,
Placed a burning coal upon it,
Gave it to his guest, the stranger,
And began to speak in this wise :
" When I blow my breath about me,

When I breathe upon the landscape,
Motionless are all the rivers,
Hard as stone becomes the water!"
　　And the young man answered, smiling
" When I blow my breath about me,
When I breathe upon the landscape,
Flowers spring up o'er all the meadows,
Singing, onward rush the rivers!"

　　" When I shake my hoary tresses,"
Said the old man darkly frowning,
" All the land with snow is covered;
All the leaves from all the branches
Fall and fade and die and wither,
For I breathe, and lo! they are not.
From the waters and the marshes
Rise the wild goose and the heron,

Fly away to distant regions,
For I speak, and lo! they are not.
And where'er my footsteps wander,
All the wild beasts of the forest
Hide themselves in holes and caverns,
And the earth becomes as flintstone!"
　　" When I shake my flowing ringlets,"
Said the young man, softly laughing,
" Showers of rain fall warm and welcome,
Plants lift up their heads rejoicing,
Back into their lakes and marshes

"Sit here by the dying embers,
Let us pass the night together"

Come the wild goose and the heron,
Homeward shoots the arrowy swallow,
Sing the bluebird and the robin,
And where'er my footsteps wander,
All the meadows wave with blossoms,
All the woodlands ring with music,
All the trees are dark with foliage!"

While they spake, the night departed:
From the distant realms of Wabun,
From his shining lodge of silver,
Like a warrior robed and painted,
Came the sun, and said, " Behold me !
Gheezis, the great sun, behold me ! "

Then the old man's tongue was speechless
And the air grew warm and pleasant,
And upon the wigwam sweetly
Sang the bluebird and the robin,
And the stream began to murmur,
And a scent of growing grasses
Through the lodge was gently wafted.

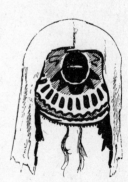

And Segwun, the youthful stranger,
More distinctly in the daylight
Saw the icy face before him;
It was Peboan, the Winter!

From his eyes the tears were flowing,
As from melting lakes the streamlets,
And his body shrunk and dwindled

As the shouting sun ascended,
Till into the air it faded,
Till into the ground it vanished,
And the young man saw before him,
On the hearth-stone of the wigwam,
Where the fire had smoked and smouldered,
Saw the earliest flower of Spring-time,
Saw the Beauty of the Spring-time,
Saw the Miskodeed in blossom.

Thus it was that in the North-land
After that unheard-of coldness,
That intolerable Winter,
Came the Spring with all its splendor,
All its birds and all its blossoms,
All its flowers and leaves and grasses.

Sailing on the wind to northward,
Flying in great flocks, like arrows,
Like huge arrows shot through heaven,
Passed the swan, the Mahnahbezee,
Speaking almost as a man speaks;
And in long lines waving, bending
Like a bow-string snapped asunder,
Came the white goose, Waw-be-wawa;
And in pairs, or singly flying,
Mahng the loon, with clangorous pinions,
The blue heron, the Shuh-shuh-gah,
And the grouse, the Mushkodasa.

In the thickets and the meadows
Piped the bluebird, the Owaissa,
On the summit of the lodges
Sang the robin, the Opechee,
In the covert of the pine-trees
Cooed the pigeon, the Omemee,
And the sorrowing Hiawatha,
Speechless in his infinite sorrow,
Heard their voices calling to him,
Went forth from his gloomy doorway,
Stood and gazed into the heaven,
Gazed upon the earth and waters.

From his wanderings far to eastward,
From the regions of the morning,
From the shining land of Wabun,
Homeward now returned Iagoo,
The great traveller, the great boaster,
Full of new and strange adventures,
Marvels many and many wonders.

And the people of the village
Listened to him as he told them
Of his marvellous adventures,
Laughing answered him in this wise :
" Ugh ! it is indeed Iagoo !
No one else beholds such wonders ! "

He had seen, he said, a water
Bigger than the Big-Sea-Water,

Broader than the Gitche Gumee,
Bitter so that none could drink it!
At each other looked the warriors,
Looked the women at each other,
Smiled, and said, " It cannot be so!
Kaw!" they said, "it cannot be so!"
  O'er it, said he, o'er this water
Came a great canoe with pinions,
A canoe with wings came flying,
Bigger than a grove of pine-trees,
Taller than the tallest tree-tops!
And the old men and the women
Looked and tittered at each other;
"Kaw!" they said, "we don't believe it!"
  From its mouth, he said, to greet him,
Came Waywassimo, the lightning,
Came the thunder, Annemeekee!
And the warriors and the women
Laughed aloud at poor Iagoo;
"Kaw!" they said, "what tales you tell us!"
  In it, said he, came a people,
In the great canoe with pinions
Came, he said, a hundred warriors;
Painted white were all their faces
And with hair their chins were covered!
And the warriors and the women
Laughed and shouted in derision,

Like the ravens on the tree-tops,
Like the crows upon the hemlocks.
" Kaw ! " they said, " what lies you tell us !
Do not think that we believe them ! "
    Only Hiawatha laughed not,
But he gravely spake and answered
To their jeering and their jesting:
" True is all Iagoo tells us ;
I have seen it in a vision,
Seen the great canoe with pinions,
Seen the people with white faces,
Seen the coming of this bearded
People of the wooden vessel
From the regions of the morning,
From the shining land of Wabun.

    " Gitche Manito, the Mighty,
The Great Spirit, the Creator,
Sends them hither on his errand,
Sends them to us with his message.
Wheresoe'er they move, before them
Swarms the stinging fly, the Ahmo,
Swarms the bee, the honey-maker ;
Wheresoe'er they tread, beneath them
Springs a flower unknown among us,
Springs the White-man's Foot in blossom.

    " Let us welcome, then, the strangers,
Hail them as our friends and brothers,

And the heart's right hand of friendship
Give them when they come to see us.
Gitche Manito, the Mighty,
Said this to me in my vision.

"I beheld, too, in that vision
All the secrets of the future,
Of the distant days that shall be.
I beheld the westward marches
Of the unknown, crowded nations.
All the land was full of people,
Restless, struggling, toiling, striving,
Speaking many tongues, yet feeling
But one heart-beat in their bosoms.
In the woodlands rang their axes,
Smoked their towns in all the valleys,
Over all the lakes and rivers
Rushed their great canoes of thunder.

"Then a darker, drearier vision
Passed before me, vague and cloud-like;
I beheld our nation scattered,
All forgetful of my counsels,
Weakened, warring with each other:
Saw the remnants of our people
Sweeping westward, wild and woful,
Like the cloud-rack of a tempest,
Like the withered leaves of Autumn!"

XXII

Hiawatha's Departure

By the shore of Gitche Gumee,
By the shining Big-Sea-Water,
At the doorway of his wigwam,
In the pleasant Summer morning,
Hiawatha stood and waited.
All the air was full of freshness,
All the earth was bright and joyous,
And before him, through the sunshine,
Westward toward the neighboring forest
Passed in golden swarms the Ahmo,

Passed the bees, the honey-makers,
Burning, singing in the sunshine.

Bright above him shone the heavens,
Level spread the lake before him;
From its bosom leaped the sturgeon,
Sparkling, flashing in the sunshine;
On its margin the great forest
Stood reflected in the water,
Every tree-top had its shadow,
Motionless beneath the water.

From the brow of Hiawatha
Gone was every trace of sorrow,
As the fog from off the water,
As the mist from off the meadow.
With a smile of joy and triumph,
With a look of exultation,
As of one who in a vision
Sees what is to be, but is not,
Stood and waited Hiawatha.

Toward the sun his hands were lifted,
Both the palms spread out against it,
And between the parted fingers
Fell the sunshine on his features,
Flecked with light his naked shoulders,
As it falls and flecks an oak-tree
Through the rifted leaves and branches.

O'er the water floating, flying,

Something in the hazy distance,
Something in the mists of morning,
Loomed and lifted from the water,
Now seemed floating, now seemed flying,
Coming nearer, nearer, nearer.
    Was it Shingebis the diver?
Or the pelican, the Shada?
Or the heron, the Shuh-shuh-gah?
Or the white goose, Waw-be-wawa,
With the water dripping, flashing,
From its glossy neck and feathers?

    It was neither goose nor diver,
Neither pelican nor heron,
O'er the water floating, flying,
Through the shining mist of morning,
But a birch canoe with paddles,
Rising, sinking on the water,
Dripping, flashing in the sunshine;
And within it came a people
From the distant land of Wabun,
From the farthest realms of morning
Came the Black-Robe chief, the Prophet,
He the Priest of Prayer, the Pale-face,
With his guides and his companions.
    And the noble Hiawatha,
With his hands aloft extended,
Held aloft in sign of welcome,

Waited, full of exultation,
Till the birch canoe with paddles
Grated on the shining pebbles,
Stranded on the sandy margin,
Till the Black-Robe chief, the Pale-face,
With the cross upon his bosom,
Landed on the sandy margin.

Then the joyous Hiawatha
Cried aloud and spake in this wise:
"Beautiful is the sun, O strangers,
When you come so far to see us!
All our town in peace awaits you,
All our doors stand open for you:
You shall enter all our wigwams,
For the heart's right hand we give you.

"Never bloomed the earth so gayly,
Never shone the sun so brightly,
As to-day they shine and blossom
When you come so far to see us!
Never was our lake so tranquil,
Nor so free from rocks and sand-bars;
For your birch canoe in passing
Has removed both rock and sand-bar.

"Never before had our tobacco
Such a sweet and pleasant flavor,
Never the broad leaves of our cornfields
Were so beautiful to look on,

Came the Black-Robe chief, . . . the Pale-face,
With his guides and his companions

As they seem to us this morning,
When you come so far to see us!"
　And the Black-Robe chief made answer,
Stammered in his speech a little,
Speaking words yet unfamiliar:
" Peace be with you, Hiawatha,
Peace be with you and your people,
Peace of prayer, and peace of pardon,
Peace of Christ, and joy of Mary!"

　Then the generous Hiawatha
Led the strangers to his wigwam,
Seated them on skins of bison,
Seated them on skins of ermine,
And the careful old Nokomis
Brought them food in bowls of basswood,
Water brought in birchen dippers,
And the calumet, the peace-pipe,
Filled and lighted for their smoking.

　All the old men of the village,
All the warriors of the nation,
All the Jossakeeds, the Prophets,
The magicians, the Wabenos,
And the medicine-men, the Medas,
Came to bid the strangers welcome;
" It is well," they said, " O brothers,
That you come so far to see us!"
　In a circle round the doorway,

With their pipes they sat in silence,
Waiting to behold the strangers,
Waiting to receive their message;
Till the Black-Robe chief, the Pale-face,
From the wigwam came to greet them,
Stammering in his speech a little,
Speaking words yet unfamiliar;
" It is well," they said, " O brother,
That you come so far to see us!"

Then the Black-Robe chief, the Prophet,
Told his message to the people,
Told the purport of his mission,
Told them of the Virgin Mary,
And her blessed Son, the Saviour,
How in distant lands and ages
He had lived on earth as we do;
How he fasted, prayed, and labored;
How the Jews, the tribe accursed,
Mocked him, scourged him, crucified him;
How he rose from where they laid him,
Walked again with his disciples,
And ascended into heaven.

And the chiefs made answer, saying:
" We have listened to your message,
We have heard your words of wisdom
We will think on what you tell us.
It is well for us, O brothers,
That you come so far to see us!"

Then they rose up and departed
Each one homeward to his wigwam,
To the young men and the women
Told the story of the strangers
Whom the Master of Life had sent them
From the shining land of Wabun.

Heavy with the heat and silence
Grew the afternoon of Summer;
With a drowsy sound the forest
Whispered round the sultry wigwam,
With a sound of sleep the water
Rippled on the beach below it;
From the cornfields shrill and ceaseless
Sang the grasshopper, Pah-puk-keena;
And the guests of Hiawatha,
Weary with the heat of Summer,
Slumbered in the sultry wigwam.

Slowly o'er the simmering landscape
Fell the evening's dusk and coolness,
And the long and level sunbeams
Shot their spears into the forest,
Breaking through its shields of shadow,
Rushed into each secret ambush,
Searched each thicket, dingle, hollow;
Still the guests of Hiawatha
Slumbered in the silent wigwam.

From his place rose Hiawatha,
Bade farewell to old Nokomis,

Spake in whispers, spake in this wise,
Did not wake the guests, that slumbered:
   "I am going, O Nokomis,
On a long and distant journey,
To the portals of the Sunset,
To the regions of the home-wind,
Of the Northwest-Wind, Keewaydin.
But these guests I leave behind me,
In your watch and ward I leave them;
See that never harm comes near them,
See that never fear molests them,
Never danger nor suspicion,
Never want of food or shelter,
In the lodge of Hiawatha!"

   Forth into the village went he,
Bade farewell to all the warriors,
Bade farewell to all the young men,
Spake persuading, spake in this wise:
   "I am going, O my people,
On a long and distant journey;
Many moons and many winters
Will have come, and will have vanished,
Ere I come again to see you.
But my guests I leave behind me;
Listen to their words of wisdom,
Listen to the truth they tell you,
For the Master of Life has sent them
From the land of light and morning!"

On the shore stood Hiawatha,
Turned and waved his hand at parting;
On the clear and luminous water
Launched his birch canoe for sailing,
From the pebbles of the margin
Shoved it forth into the water;
Whispered to it, "Westward! westward!"
And with speed it darted forward.

And the evening sun descending
Set the clouds on fire with redness,
Burned the broad sky, like a prairie,
Left upon the level water
One long track and trail of splendor,
Down whose stream, as down a river,
Westward, westward Hiawatha
Sailed into the fiery sunset,
Sailed into the purple vapors,
Sailed into the dusk of evening.

And the people from the margin
Watched him floating, rising, sinking,
Till the birch canoe seemed lifted
High into that sea of splendor,
Till it sank into the vapors
Like the new moon slowly, slowly
Sinking in the purple distance.

And they said, "Farewell forever!"
Said, "Farewell, O Hiawatha!"
And the forests, dark and lonely,

Moved through all their depths of darkness,
Sighed, "Farewell, O Hiawatha!"
And the waves upon the margin
Rising, rippling on the pebbles,
Sobbed, "Farewell, O Hiawatha!"
And the heron, the Shuh-shuh-gah,
From her haunts among the fen-lands,
Screamed, "Farewell, O Hiawatha!"
  Thus departed Hiawatha,
Hiawatha the Beloved,
In the glory of the sunset,
In the purple mists of evening,
To the regions of the home-wind,
Of the Northwest-Wind, Keewaydin,
To the Islands of the Blessed,
To the kingdom of Ponemah,
To the land of the Hereafter!

Vocabulary and Notes

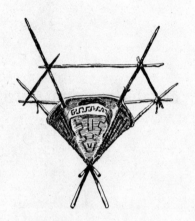

Vocabulary and Notes

THIS Indian Edda — if I may so call it — is founded
on a tradition, prevalent among the North American
Indians, of a personage of miraculous birth, who was
sent among them to clear their rivers, forests, and fishing-grounds, and to teach them the arts of peace. He
was known among different tribes by the several names
of Michabou, Chiabo, Manabozo, Tarenya-wagon, and
Hiawatha.   Mr. Schoolcraft gives an account of him in
his *Algic Researches*, vol. i. p. 134 ; and in his *History,
Condition, and Prospects of the Indian Tribes of the
United States*, Part III. p. 314, may be found the Iro-
quois form of the tradition, derived from the verbal
narrations of an Onondaga chief.

Into this old tradition I have woven other curious Indian legends, drawn chiefly from the various and valuable writings of Mr. Schoolcraft, to whom the literary world is greatly indebted for his indefatigable zeal in rescuing from oblivion so much of the legendary lore of the Indians.

The scene of the poem is among the Ojibways on the southern shore of Lake Superior, in the region between the Pictured Rocks and the Grand Sable.

VOCABULARY.

Adjidau'mo, *the red squirrel.*
Ahdeek', *the reindeer.*
Ahkose'win, *fever.*
Ahmeek', *the beaver.*
Algon'quin, *Ojibway.*
Annemee'kee, *the thunder.*
Apuk'wa, *a bulrush.*
Baim-wa'wa, *the sound of the thunder.*
Bemah'gut, *the grapevine.*
Be'na, *the pheasant.*
Big-Sea-Water, *Lake Superior.*
Bukada'win, *famine.*
Cheemaun', *a birch canoe.*
Chetowaik', *the plover.*
Chibia'bos, *a musician; friend of Hiawatha; ruler in the Land of Spirits.*
Dahin'da, *the bull-frog.*
Dush-kwo-ne'she, *or* Kwo-ne'she, *the dragon-fly.*
Esa, *shame upon you.*
Ewa-yea', *lullaby.*
Ghee'zis, *the sun.*
Gitche Gu'mee, *the Big-Sea-Water, Lake Superior.*
Gitche Man'ito, *the Great Spirit, the Master of Life.*
Gushkewau', *the darkness.*
Hiawa'tha, *the Wise Man, the Teacher; son of Mudjekeewis, the West-Wind, and Wenonah, daughter of Nokomis.*
Ia'goo, *a great boaster and story-teller.*
Inin'ewug, *men, or pawns in the Game of the Bowl.*
Ishkoodah', *fire; a comet.*
Jee'bi, *a ghost, a spirit.*
Joss'akeed, *a prophet.*

Kabibonok´ka, *the North-Wind.*

Kagh, *the hedgehog.*

Ka´go, *do not.*

Kahgahgee´, *the raven.*

Kaw, *no.*

Kaween´, *no indeed.*

Kayoshk´, *the sea-gull.*

Kee´go, *a fish.*

Keeway´din, *the Northwest-Wind, the Home-Wind.*

Kena´beek, *a serpent.*

Keneu´, *the great war-eagle.*

Keno´zha, *the pickerel.*

Ko´ko-ko´ho, *the owl.*

Kuntasoo´, *the Game of Plum-stones.*

Kwa´sind, *the Strong Man.*

Kwo-ne´she, *or* Dush-kwo-ne´she, *the dragon-fly.*

Mahnahbe´zee, *the swan.*

Mahng, *the loon.*

Mahn-go-tay´see, *loon-hearted brave.*

Mahnomo´nee, *wild rice.*

Ma´ma, *the woodpecker.*

Maskeno´zha, *the pike.*

Me´da, *a medicine-man.*

Meenah´ga, *the blueberry.*

Megissog´won, *the great Pearl-Feather, a magician and the Manito of Wealth.*

Meshinau´wa, *a pipe-bearer.*

Minjekah´wun, *Hiawatha's mittens.*

Minneha´ha, *Laughing Water; a waterfall on a stream running into the Mississippi, between Fort Snelling and the Falls of St. Anthony.*

Minneha´ha, *Laughing Water; wife of Hiawatha.*

Minne-wa´wa, *a pleasant sound, as of the wind in the trees.*

Mishe-Mo´kwa, *the Great Bear.*

Mishe-Nah´ma, *the Great Sturgeon.*

Miskodeed´, *the Spring Beauty, the Claytonia Virginica.*

Monda´min, *Indian Corn.*

Moon of Bright Nights, *April.*

Moon of Leaves, *May.*

Moon of Strawberries, *June.*

Moon of the Falling Leaves, *September.*

Moon of Snow-Shoes, *November.*

Mudjekee´wis, *the West-Wind; father of Hiawatha.*

Mudway-aush´ka, *sound of waves on a shore.*

Mushkoda´sa, *the grouse.*

Na′gow Wud′joo, *the Sand Dunes of Lake Superior.*
Nah′ma, *the sturgeon.*
Nah′ma-wusk, *spearmint.*
Nee-ba-naw′baigs, *water spirits.*
Nenemoo′sha, *sweetheart.*
Nepah′win, *sleep.*
Noko′mis, *a grandmother ; mother of Wenonah.*
No′sa, *my father.*
Nush′ka, *look ! look !*
Odah′min, *the strawberry.*
Okahah′wis, *the fresh-water herring.*
Ome′mee, *the pigeon.*
Ona′gon, *a bowl.*
Onaway′, *awake.*
Ope′chee, *the robin.*
Osse′o, *Son of the Evening Star.*
Owais′sa, *the bluebird.*
Oweenee′, *wife of Osseo.*
Ozawa′beek, *a round piece of brass or copper in the Game of the Bowl.*
Pah-puk-kee′na, *the grasshopper.*
Pau′guk, *death.*
Pau-Puk-Kee′wis, *the handsome Yenadizze, the Storm-Fool.*
Pauwa′ting, *Sault Sainte Marie.*
Pe′boan, *Winter.*
Pem′ican, *meat of the deer or buffalo dried and pounded.*
Pezheekee′, *the bison.*
Pishnekuh′, *the brant.*
Pone′mah, *hereafter.*
Pugasaing′, *Game of the Bowl.*
Puggawau′gun, *a war-club.*
Puk-Wudj′ies, *little wild men of the woods ; pygmies.*
Sah-sah-je′wun, *rapids.*
Sah′wa, *the perch.*
Segwun′, *Spring.*
Sha′da, *the pelican.*
Shahbo′min, *the gooseberry.*
Shah-shah, *long ago.*
Shaugoda′ya, *a coward.*
Shawgashee′, *the craw-fish.*
Shawonda′see, *the South-Wind.*
Shaw-shaw, *the swallow.*
Shesh′ebwug, *ducks ; pieces in the Game of the Bowl.*
Shin′gebis, *the diver or grebe.*
Showain′ neme′shin, *pity me.*

Shuh-shuh′gah, *the blue heron.*
Soan-ge-ta′ha, *strong hearted.*
Subbeka′she, *the spider.*
Sugge′ma, *the mosquito.*
To′tem, *family coat of arms.*
Ugh, *yes.*
Ugudwash′, *the sun-fish.*
Unktahee′, *the God of Water.*
Wabas′so, *the rabbit ; the North.*
Wabe′no, *a magician, a juggler.*
Wabe′no-wusk, *yarrow.*
Wa-bun, *the East-Wind.*
Wa′bun An′nung, *the Star of the East, the Morning Star.*
Wahono′win, *a cry of lamentation.*
Wah-wah-tay′see, *the fire-fly.*
Wam′pum, *beads of shell.*
Waubewy′on, *a white skin wrapper.*
Wa′wa, *the wild goose.*
Waw′beek, *a rock.*
Waw-be-wa′wa, *the white goose.*
Wawonais′sa, *the whippoorwill.*
Way-muk-kwa′na, *the caterpillar.*
Wen′digoes, *giants.*
Weno′nah, *Hiawatha's mother, daughter of Nokomis.*
Yenadiz′ze, *an idler and gambler ; an Indian dandy.*

["Suddenly and immensely popular in this country, greatly admired by many foreign critics, imitated with perfect ease by any clever school-boy, serving as a model for metrical advertisements, made fun of, sneered at, abused, admired, but, at any rate, a picture full of pleasing fancies and melodious cadences. The very names are jewels which the most fastidious muse might be proud to wear. Coming from the realm of the Androscoggin and of Moosetukmaguntuk, how could he have found two such delicious names as Hiawatha and Minnehaha? The eight-syllable trochaic verse of *Hiawatha*, like the eight-syllable iambic verse of *The Lady of the Lake*, and others of Scott's poems, has a fatal facility, which I have elsewhere endeavored to explain on physiological principles. The recital of each line

uses up the air of one natural expiration, so that we read, as we naturally do, eighteen or twenty lines in a minute, without disturbing the normal rhythm of breathing, which is also eighteen or twenty breaths to the minute. The standing objection to this is, that it makes the octo-syllabic verse too easy writing and too slipshod reading. Yet in this most frequently criticised composition the poet has shown a subtle sense of the requirements of his simple story of a primitive race, in choosing the most fluid of measures, that lets the thought run through it in easy sing-song, such as oral tradition would be sure to find on the lips of the story-tellers of the wigwam." — Oliver Wendell Holmes : *Remarks at meeting of Massachusetts Historical Society*, April 13, 1882.]

Page 3. *In the Vale of Tawasentha.*

This valley, now called Norman's Kill, is in Albany County, New York.

Page 6. *On the Mountains of the Prairie.*

Mr. Catlin, in his *Letters and Notes on the Manners, Customs, and Condition of the North American Indians*, vol. ii. p. 160, gives an interesting account of the *Côteau des Prairies*, and the Red Pipestone Quarry. He says : —

" Here (according to their traditions) happened the mysterious birth of the red pipe, which has blown its fumes of peace and war to the remotest corners of the continent; which has visited every warrior, and passed through its reddened stem the irrevocable oath of war and desolation. And here, also, the peace-breathing calumet was born, and fringed with the eagle's quills, which has shed its thrilling fumes over the land, and soothed the fury of the relentless savage.

" The Great Spirit at an ancient period here called the Indian nations together, and, standing on the precipice of the red pipe-stone rock, broke from its wall a piece, and made a huge pipe by turning it in his hand, which he smoked over them, and to the North, the South, the East, and the West, and told them that this stone was red, — that it was their flesh, — that they must use it for their pipes of peace, — that it belonged to them all, and that the war-club and scalping-knife must not be raised on its ground. At the last whiff of his pipe his head went into a great cloud, and the whole surface of the rock for several miles was melted and glazed; two great ovens were opened beneath, and two women (guardian spirits of the place) entered them in a blaze of fire; and they are heard there yet (Tso-mec-cos-tee and Tso-me-cos-te-won-dee), answering to the invocations of the high-priests or medicine-men, who consult them when they are visitors to this sacred place.".

Page 15. *Hark you, Bear! you are a coward.*

This anecdote is from Heckewelder. In his account of the Indian Nations, he describes an Indian hunter as addressing a bear in nearly these words. "I was present," he says, "at the delivery of this curious invective; when the hunter had despatched the bear, I asked him how he thought that poor animal could understand what he said to it. 'Oh,' said he in answer, 'the bear understood me very well; did you not observe how *ashamed* he looked while I was upbraiding him?'" — *Transactions of the American Philosophical Society*, vol. i. p. 240.

Page 28. *Hush! the Naked Bear will hear thee!*

Heckewelder, in a letter published in the *Transactions of the American Philosophical Society*, vol. iv. p. 260, speaks of this tradition as prevalent among the Mohicans and Delawares.

"Their reports," he says, "run thus: that among all animals that had been formerly in this country, this was the most ferocious; that it was much larger than the largest of the common bears, and remarkably long-bodied; all over (except a spot of hair on its back of a white color) naked. . . .

"The history of this animal used to be a subject of

conversation among the Indians, especially when in the woods a hunting. I have also heard them say to their children when crying: 'Hush! the naked bear will hear you, be upon you, and devour you.'"

Page 45. *Where the Falls of Minnehaha*, etc.

"The scenery about Fort Snelling is rich in beauty. The Falls of St. Anthony are familiar to travelers, and to readers of Indian sketches. Between the fort and these falls are the 'Little Falls,' forty feet in height, on a stream that empties into the Mississippi. The Indians called them Minehah-hah, or 'laughing waters.'" — Mrs. Eastman's *Dacotah, or Legends of the Sioux*, Introd. p. ii.

Page 111. *Sand Hills of the Nagow Wudjoo.*

A description of the *Grand Sable*, or great sand-dunes of Lake Superior, is given in Foster and Whitney's *Report on the Geology of the Lake Superior Land District*, Part II. p. 131.

"The Grand Sable possesses a scenic interest little inferior to that of the Pictured Rocks. The explorer passes abruptly from a coast of consolidated sand to one of loose materials; and although in the one case the cliffs are less precipitous, yet in the other they attain a higher altitude. He sees before him a long reach of coast, resembling a vast sand-bank, more than three hundred and fifty feet in height, without a trace of vegetation. Ascending to the top, rounded hillocks of blown sand are observed, with occasional clumps of trees, standing out like oases in the desert."

Page 112. *Onaway! Awake, beloved!*

The original of this song may be found it *Littell's Living Age*, vol. xxv. p. 45.

Page 117. *Or the Red Swan floating, flying.*

The fanciful tradition of the Red Swan may be found in Schoolcraft's *Algic Researches*, vol. ii. p. 9. Three brothers were hunting on a wager to see who would bring home the first game.

" They were to shoot no other animal," so the legend
says, " but such as each was in the habit of killing.
They set out different ways; Odjibwa, the youngest,
had not gone far before he saw a bear, an animal he
was not to kill, by the agreement. He followed him
close, and drove an arrow through him, which brought
him to the ground. Although contrary to the bet, he
immediately commenced skinning him, when suddenly
something red tinged all the air around him. He
rubbed his eyes, thinking he was perhaps deceived; but
without effect, for the red hue continued. At length he
heard a strange noise at a distance. It first appeared
like a human voice, but after following the sound for
some distance, he reached the shores of a lake, and soon
saw the object he was looking for. At a distance out
in the lake sat a most beautiful Red Swan, whose plumage glittered in the sun, and who would now and then
make the same noise he had heard. He was within
long bow-shot, and, pulling the arrow from the bow-
string up to his ear, took deliberate aim and shot. The
arrow took no effect; and he shot and shot again till
his quiver was empty. Still the swan remained, moving round and round, stretching its long neck and dip-
ping its bill into the water, as if heedless of the arrows
shot at it. Odjibwa ran home and got all his own and
his brothers' arrows, and shot them all away. He then
stood and gazed at the beautiful bird. While standing,
he remembered his brothers' saying that in their de-
ceased father's medicine-sack were three magic arrows.
Off he started, his anxiety to kill the swan overcoming
all scruples. At any other time he would have deemed
it sacrilege to open his father's medicine-sack; but now
he hastily seized the three arrows and ran back, leaving
the other contents of the sack scattered over the lodge.
The swan was still there. He shot the first arrow with
great precision, and came very near to it. The second
came still closer; as he took the last arrow, he felt his

arm firmer, and, drawing it up with vigor, saw it pass through the neck of the swan a little above the breast. Still it did not prevent the bird from flying off, which it did, however, at first slowly, flapping its wings and rising gradually into the air, and then flying off toward the sinking of the sun." — Pages 10–12.

Page 130. *When I think of my beloved.*

The original of this song may be found in *Oneóta*, p. 15.

Page 132. *Sing the mysteries of Mondamin.*

The Indians hold the maize, or Indian corn, in great veneration. "They esteem it so important and divine a grain," says Schoolcraft, "that their story-tellers invented various tales, in which this idea is symbolized under the form of a special gift from the Great Spirit. The Odjibwa-Algonquins, who call it Mon-da-min, that is, this Spirit's grain or berry, have a pretty story of the kind, in which the stalk in full tassel is represented as descending from the sky, under the guise of a handsome youth, in answer to the prayers of a young man at his fast of virility, or coming to manhood.

" It is well known that corn-planting and corn-gathering, at least among all the still *uncolonized* tribes, are left entirely to the females and children, and a few superannuated old men. It is not generally known, perhaps, that this labor is not compulsory, and that it is assumed by the females as a just equivalent, in their view, for the onerous and continuous labor of the other sex, in providing meats, and skins for clothing, by the chase, and in defending their villages against their enemies, and keeping intruders off their territories. A good Indian housewife deems this a part of her prerogative, and prides herself to have a store of corn to exercise her hospitality, or duly honor her husband's hospitality in the entertainment of the lodge guests." — *Oneóta*, p. 82.

Page 134. *Thus the fields shall be more fruitful.*

" A singular proof of this belief, in both sexes, of the mysterious influence of the steps of a woman on the vegetable and insect creation, is found in an ancient custom, which was related to me, respecting corn-planting. It was the practice of the hunter's wife, when the field of corn had been planted, to choose the first dark or overclouded evening to perform a secret circuit, *sans habillement*, around the field. For this purpose she slipped out of the lodge in the evening, unobserved, to some obscure nook, where she completely disrobed. Then, taking her matchecota, or principal garment, in one hand, she dragged it around the field. This was thought to insure a prolific crop, and to prevent the assaults of insects and worms upon the grain. It was supposed they could not creep over the charmed line." — *Oneóta*, p. 83.

Page 138. *With his prisoner-string he bound him.*

" These cords," says Mr. Tanner, " are made of the bark of the elm-tree, by boiling and then immersing it in cold water. . . . The leader of a war party commonly carries several fastened about his waist, and if, in the course of the fight, any one of his young men takes a prisoner, it is his duty to bring him immediately to the chief, to be tied, and the latter is responsible for his safe-keeping." — *Narrative of Captivity and Adventures*, p. 412.

Page 141.

Wagemin, the thief of cornfields,
Paimosaid, who steals the maize-ear.

" If one of the young female huskers finds a *red* ear of corn, it is typical of a brave admirer, and is regarded as a fitting present to some young warrior. But if the ear be *crooked*, and tapering to a point, no matter what color, the whole circle is set in a roar, and *wa-ge-min* is the word shouted aloud. It is the symbol of a thief in the cornfield. It is considered as the image of an old man stooping as he enters the lot. Had the chisel of

Praxiteles been employed to produce this image, it could not more vividly bring to the minds of the merry group the idea of a pilferer of their favorite mondámin. . . .

"The literal meaning of the term is, a mass, or crooked ear of grain ; but the ear of corn so called is a conventional type of a little old man pilfering ears of corn in a cornfield. It is in this manner that a single word or term, in these curious languages, becomes the fruitful parent of many ideas. And we can thus perceive why it is that the word *wagemin* is alone competent to excite merriment in the husking circle.

"This term is taken as a basis of the cereal chorus, or corn song, as sung by the Northern Algonquin tribes. It is coupled with the phrase *Paimosaid*,— a permutative form of the Indian substantive, made from the verb *pim-o-sa*, to walk. Its literal meaning is, *he who walks*, or *the walker ;* but the ideas conveyed by it are, he who walks by night to pilfer corn. It offers, therefore, a kind of paralleism in expression to the preceding term." — *Oneóta*, p. 254.

Page 161. *Pagasaing, with thirteen pieces.*

This Game of the Bowl is the principal game of hazard among the Northern tribes of Indians. Mr. Schoolcraft gives a particular account of it in *Oneóta*, p. 85. "This game," he says, "is very fascinating to some portions of the Indians. They stake at it their ornaments, weapons, clothing, canoes, horses, everything in fact they possess ; and have been known, it is said, to set up their wives and children, and even to forfeit their own liberty. Of such desperate stakes I have seen no examples, nor do I think the game itself in common use. It is rather confined to certain persons, who hold the relative rank of gamblers in Indian society, — men who are not noted as hunters or warriors, or steady providers for their families. Among these are persons who bear the term of *Ienadizze-wug*, that is, wanderers about the country, braggadocios, or fops. It can hardly

be classed with the popular games of amusement, by which skill and dexterity are acquired. I have generally found the chiefs and graver men of the tribes, who encouraged the young men to play ball, and are sure to be present at the customary sports, to witness, and sanction, and applaud them, speak lightly and disparagingly of this game of hazard. Yet it cannot be denied that some of the chiefs, distinguished in war and the chase, at the West, can be referred to as lending their example to its fascinating power."

See also his *History, Conditions, and Prospects of the Indian Tribes*, Part II. p. 72.

Page 181. *To the Pictured Rocks of sandstone.*

The reader will find a long description of the Pictured Rocks in Foster and Whitney's *Report on the Geology of the Lake Superior Land District*, Part II. p. 124. From this I make the following extract : —

"The Pictured Rocks may be described, in general terms, as a series of sandstone bluffs extending along the shore of Lake Superior for about five miles, and rising, in most places, vertically from the water, without any beach at the base, to a height varying from fifty to nearly two hundred feet. Were they simply a line of cliffs, they might not, so far as relates to height or extent, be worthy of a rank among great natural curiosities, although such an assemblage of rocky strata, washed by the waves of the great lake, would not, under any circumstances, be destitute of grandeur. To the voyager, coasting along their base in his frail canoe, they would, at all times, be an object of dread ; the recoil of the surf, the rock-bound coast, affording for miles no place of refuge, — the lowering sky, the rising wind, — all these would excite his apprehension, and induce him to ply a vigorous oar until the dreaded wall was passed. But in the Pictured Rocks there are two features which communicate to the scenery a wonderful and almost unique character. These are, first, the curious manner

in which the cliffs have been excavated and worn away by the action of the lake, which, for centuries, has dashed an ocean-like surf against their base; and, second, the equally curious manner in which large portions of the surface have been colored by bands of brilliant hues.

"It is from the latter circumstance that the name, by which these cliffs are known to the American traveller, is derived; while that applied to them by the French voyageurs ('Les Portails') is derived from the former, and by far the most striking peculiarity.

"The term *Pictured Rocks* has been in use for a great length of time; but when it was first applied, we have been unable to discover. It would seem that the first travellers were more impressed with the novel and striking distribution of colors on the surface than with the astonishing variety of form into which the cliffs themselves have been worn. . . .

"Our voyageurs had many legends to relate of the pranks of the *Menni-bojou* in these caverns, and, in answer to our inquiries, seemed disposed to fabricate stories, without end, of the achievements of this Indian deity."

Page 218. *Toward the sun his hands were lifted.*

In this manner, and with such salutations, was Father Marquette received by the Illinois. See his *Voyages et Découvertes*, Section V.